CULTURES OF THE WORLD

Kazakhstan

Guek-Cheng Pang

Marshall Cavendish
Benchmark
New York

PICTURE CREDITS
Cover: ©Sean Gallup / Getty Images
Audrius Tomonis: 138 • Corbis: 28, 34, 38, 77, 78, 93, 94, 119, 124 • Getty Images: 11, 84, 131 • Lonely Planet
Images: 44, 53, 85, 92, 96, 104, 127, 129 • North Wind Pictures Archives: 21, 22, 23, 24, 25 • Photolibrary: 1,
3, 5, 6, 8, 12, 13, 14, 15, 16, 17, 18, 19, 20, 26, 27, 30, 31, 32, 35, 40, 41, 42, 46, 48, 49, 50, 51, 52, 54, 56, 57, 58,
59, 60, 61, 62, 63, 64, 67, 68, 69, 71, 72, 73, 74, 75, 79, 80, 81, 86, 87, 88, 89, 90, 95, 97, 98, 99, 100, 101, 102,
105, 106, 107, 108, 109, 110, 111, 113, 114, 116, 118, 122, 123, 128, 130 • Reuters / Shamil Zhumatov / Archive
Photos: 66 • Trip Photographic Library: 7, 9, 10, 29, 33, 37, 45, 47, 76, 82, 83, 115, 125, 126

PRECEDING PAGE
Beautiful icicles frame the natural nooks at the Tien Shan mountain range in Kazakhstan.

Publisher (U.S.): Michelle Bisson
Editors: Deborah Grahame-Smith, Mindy Pang
Copyreader: Tara Tomczyk
Designers: Nancy Sabato, Steven Tan
Cover picture researcher: Tracey Engel
Picture researcher: Thomas Khoo

Marshall Cavendish Benchmark
99 White Plains Road
Tarrytown, NY 10591
Website: www.marshallcavendish.us

© Times Media Private Limited 2001
© Marshall Cavendish International (Asia) Private Limited 2011
® "Cultures of the World" is a registered trademark of Times Publishing Limited.

Originated and designed by Times Media Private Limited
An imprint of Marshall Cavendish International (Asia) Private Limited
A member of Times Publishing Limited

Marshall Cavendish is a trademark of Times Publishing Limited.

Library of Congress Cataloging-in-Publication Data
Pang, Guek-Cheng, 1950-
  Kazakhstan / Guek-Cheng Pang
     p. cm. — (Cultures of the world)
  Includes bibliographical references and index.
  Summary: "Provides comprehensive information on the geography, history,
    wildlife, governmental structure, economy, cultural diversity, peoples,
    religion, and culture of Kazakhstan"--Provided by publisher.
  ISBN 978-1-60870-455-2
  1. Kazakhstan—Juvenile literature. I. Title.
  DK903.C49 2011
  958.45—dc22   2010030341

Printed in China
7 6 5 4 3 2 1

CONTENTS

INTRODUCTION

AT DIFFERENT TIMES IN THE PAST, HUNS, TURKS, AND MONGOLS fought among themselves in Central Asia. When the fighting subsided in the 15th century, a people who prided themselves on being different emerged. They called themselves Kazakhs—independent and free wanderers. By the second half of the 19th century, however, Kazakhstan became a colony of the Russian Empire. Although it was beneficial in some respects, it still led to detrimental phenomena such as being forced into sedentary life and famines. The limitations on the nomadic lifestyle began during the Russian Empire and the process was intensified later, when Kazakhstan was a republic in the Soviet Union, during which time the Kazakhs were forced into a sedentary lifestyle. The Kazakhs watched as their lands were forcibly taken away and ruined and their customs and traditions suppressed. Their country became the dumping ground of millions of people, so much so that they became a minority in their own land. Fortunately, with the breakup of the Soviet Union in 1991, Kazakhstan gained independence. The challenge for Kazakhs today is to develop a cohesive national identity, in the process rediscovering their culture, to manage their vast land rich in natural resources, and to strengthen their relationships with neighboring nations.

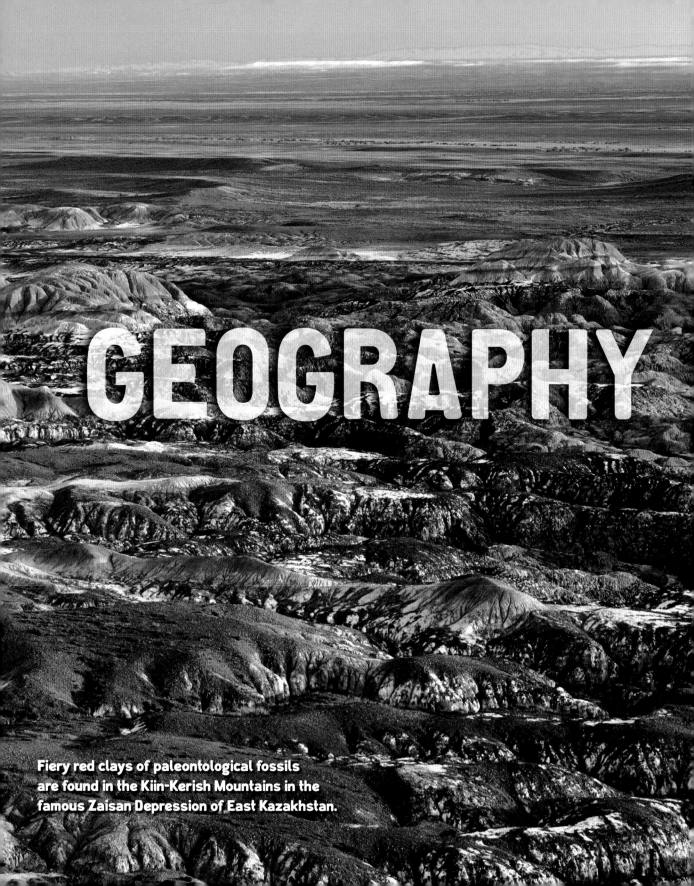

GEOGRAPHY

Fiery red clays of paleontological fossils are found in the Kiin-Kerish Mountains in the famous Zaisan Depression of East Kazakhstan.

CHAPTER 1

AZAKHSTAN IS A LARGE, landlocked country in the middle of Central Asia. Its area is 1,052,089 square miles (2,724,900 square kilometers), almost four times the size of Texas.

From the Ural Mountains in the north to the bordering countries of Uzbekistan and Kyrgyzstan in the south, it measures 1,242 miles (2,000 km). From the border with China in the east to the shores of the Caspian Sea in the west, the distance is 1,863 miles (3,000 km) wide.

An unusual rock formation in Lake Borovoye.

Kazakhstan is the ninth-largest country and the largest landlocked country in the world. The only countries larger than Kazakhstan are Russia, Canada, China, the United States, Brazil, Australia, India, and Argentina.

The undulating hills of Kazakhstan. Kazakhstan is the largest state in Central Asia and the ninth-largest country in the world.

Kazakhstan used to be a part of the Soviet Union before its breakup in 1991. Today Kazakhstan's population of 15.4 million makes it the third most populous republic in the Commonwealth of Independent States (CIS), which includes Armenia, Azerbaijan, Belarus, Georgia, Kyrgyzstan, Moldova, the Russian Federation, Tajikistan, Turkmenistan, the Ukraine, and Uzbekistan.

VARIED LANDSCAPES

About 44 percent of Kazakhstan is desert, while 9 percent of the country consists of mixed prairie and forest or treeless prairie. Mountainous regions form 12.4 percent of the landscape. The Tien Shan mountain chain, lying along the border of Kazakhstan, Kyrgyzstan, and China, rises mightily in the southeast. The Altai (or Altay) mountain system, with three distinctive ridges, is in the northeast. Also in the east is Lake Balkhash, a huge, shallow pool that is distinctive because the eastern half is salty, while the western half consists of fresh water. Farther inland are the Chingiz-Tau Mountains, rising to about 5,000 feet (1,523 meters). The Caspian Depression, a dominant feature in the west and southwest, is as much as 95 feet (29 m) below sea level at its lowest point. South of the depression are the Ustyurt Plateau and Tupqaraghan Peninsula, which borders the Caspian Sea. The Greater Barsuki Desert and the Kyzylkum Desert are located near the Aral

Sea, while the Muyunkum Desert and the Betpaqdala Desert lies in south-central Kazakhstan.

RICHES BENEATH THE LAND

In the north the landscape is a mixture of forests and steppe. This is the most fertile region in the country, although the soil system is very fragile. It is also the most heavily cultivated and agriculturally most productive region. As one travels south the grasslands change to desert and semi-desert areas. Unsuitable for agriculture, the deserts are vast, empty, and desolate, and little has changed since the days when Genghis Khan and his Mongol hordes swept through Central Asia. But underneath this apparent wasteland lie huge reserves of oil, gas, and other rich mineral resources.

SNOW-COVERED MOUNTAINS

In the east and southeast, the rich lowlands give way to hills and foothills, eventually rising to the Tien Shan and Altai mountain ranges that Kazakhstan shares with its neighbors China and Russia. Kazakhstan's most beautiful scenery can be found in this region.

Steppes account for about 26 percent of the total land area of Kazakhstan.

Many of the peaks in the Tien Shan and Altai ranges are snow-covered all year.

The Tien Shan Mountains (the name means "Heavenly Mountains" in Chinese) are the major mountain system in Central Asia. It stretches over 1,490 miles (2,400 km), through China, Kyrgyzstan, and Kazakhstan. The highest point in Kazakhstan, the 22,958-foot (6,995-m) Peak Khan-Tengri, is located in the Tien Shan range, but it is not the highest peak in these mountains. That is Peak Pobedy—Russian for "victory"—which rises to 24,415 feet (7,439 m) in eastern Kyrgyzstan. The Altai Mountains are a gentle range, with more woods and meadows than rocks and ravines.

RIVERS AND LAKES

Many of Kazakhstan's rivers have their source in these mountain ranges. Except for the Tobyl, Ishim (Esil), and Irtysh (Ertis) rivers that flow into the Arctic Ocean after joining the Ob River in Russia, the rest of the rivers flow into the Caspian and Aral seas or disappear into the deserts and steppes. Many of the 7,000 streams are seasonal and evaporate in the summer.

One can distinguish three major river systems. In the west the Ural and Emba rivers flow through the Caspian Depression before ending their journey in the Caspian Sea. In the southeast several rivers flow out of the highlands. Of these, the largest rivers are the Chu and the Syr Darya. The Chu ends in the Muyunkum Desert and the Betpaqdala Basin. The Syr Darya empties into the Aral Sea. The third system flows from the Tien Shan Mountains into Lake Balkhash. The Ili and Ayaguz rivers are the largest in this system.

Kazakhstan has 48,000 lakes, but most of these have an area of less than a square mile (2.6 square km). Those in the lowlands and the deserts are usually salty lakes, while those in the north and in the mountains are fed with fresh water from the snow. The Caspian and Aral seas and Lake Balkhash are the three largest bodies of water in the country.

CLIMATE

A landlocked country located at a great distance from the sea, Kazakhstan has a continental climate. This means it is affected by the large land masses surrounding it rather than oceans. It is very cold in the winter, especially in the north, where temperatures can drop to -58°F (-50°C). In the summer, especially in the southern deserts, it can be as hot as 113°F (45°C).

Autumn in Almaty. The land experiences extreme seasonal changes, with harsh winters and scorching summers.

Kazakhstan is also a dry country, especially in the south-central region, which receives only about 4 inches (10 centimeters) of rain annually. The country is so far inland that moisture-laden ocean winds drop their rainwater long before they reach Kazakhstan. The lack of rain means that most days are sunny and the skies are often blue and cloudless. The wettest part of the country is in the mountainous eastern region, which gets as much as 24 inches (61 cm) of precipitation a year, mainly in the form of snow.

FLORA AND FAUNA

Kazakhstan is rich in flora and fauna. Eight nature reserves have been established to try to protect the uniqueness of the land. There are more than 6,000 species of plants, of which 535 are found only in Kazakhstan. About 155 species of mammals, 480 species of birds, and 150 species of fish add to the diversity.

Fir trees laced with powdery-soft snow in the Zailisky Alatau Mountains in Almaty.

The golden eagle is one of Kazakhstan's national symbols and appears on the national flag. Kazakhs revere the eagle as a symbol of power and strength because it is the master of the skies. The female bird is larger than the male, measuring 3 feet (1 m) from beak to tail. The eagle has a wingspan of 7 feet (2 m). Its overall color is dark brown, but the feathers over the back of the head and neck are a distinct golden color, hence its name. Golden eagles nest in the high, mountainous country on cliff ledges and in the tops of tall trees. They can also be found in the mountainous regions in the northwestern United States, Canada, and Mexico.

The country has few forests; it is mostly grassland, with dry shrubby wormwood, Russian thistle, black saxaul, and tamarisk growing on the plains and in the deserts and feather grass on the drier plains. Nauryzym Nature Reserve in the Kostanay region was established in 1934 to protect the pine forests there. The area shelters several rare animals such as the mouflon, a kind of wild sheep; the long-needled hedgehog; wildcats such as the caracal and barkhan, or sand cat; and the beautiful bustard, a game bird.

The Tien Shan Mountains are home to the endangered snow leopard, Tien Shan brown bear, Siberian stag, bearded vulture with a wingspan of over 10 feet (3 m), Himalayan ular or mountain turkey-hen, and golden eagle, a favorite bird of Kazakh hunters. In the Altai Mountains can be found the giant Siberian stag, also called an elik, and the small musk deer. Lake Alakol in the southeast is a nature reserve and is the habitat for rare birds such as the fish hawk and the black stork.

In his presentation speech, President Nazarbayev explained that the capital was moved to Astana because it was, he said, on the Sary-Arka steppe, placing it not only in the center of the country but also in the center of the Eurasian continent.

The fresh and saltwater lakes of the steppes attract all kinds of migrating birds. In addition there are numerous species of ducks, geese, herons, gulls, sandpipers, and terns. Lake Tengiz in central Kazakhstan attracts millions of migratory birds every year and hosts the northernmost nesting colony of pink flamingos that make their nests here. Birds of prey circle the skies— eagles, merlins, kestrels, and others. Large herds of Saiga antelope and elk roam the plains.

The deserts are home to hordes of Middle Asian gazelle. There are also many species of jerboas, polecats, and birds such as the jay, lark, and desert dove. One of the world's largest lizards, the gray monitor lizard, lives in the Kyzylkum Desert. There are many other species of lizards and snakes.

Fishermen catch sturgeon, trout, carp, herring, and roach in the seas, rivers, and lakes. The sheatfish, a type of catfish that can grow to more than 6.6 feet (2 m) long and weigh more than 440 pounds (200 kilograms), is a game fish sought by anglers fishing in the Ili river system.

The singing dunes of the desert landscape in Altyn Emel National Park. The whistling sound may be caused by wind passing over the sand.

MAJOR CITIES AND TOWNS

Before the 20th century Kazakhstan had few large cities. The Kazakhs were nomads and lived in yurts, which are tent-like structures, or in small villages that centered on farming or that were located on trade routes. After World War II an influx of Russian industrial workers resulted in a rapid growth of cities. Now more than half the population lives in cities.

The towns are small settlements or villages separated by large areas of cultivated land in the north or inhospitable plains and deserts in the south. Typical Soviet-planned towns, such as Karangandy and Oskemen, have straight, wide streets that are bordered by nondescript gray buildings several stories high and surrounded by industrial zones.

ASTANA The town of Akmola was renamed Astana (which means "capital" in Kazakh) and made the capital of the country in May 1998 by a decree of the president of the republic, Nursultan Nazarbayev.

The Kay Munay Gaz building and the Bayterek monument are the cultural landmarks of modern Astana. Astana has a long history, as it was located along the old Steppe Route that was in use long before the famous Silk Road.

An aerial view of Almaty, the country's cultural center, in the shadow of the Zailisky Alatau Mountains. The city houses many museums and theaters.

Astana has undergone several name changes. It was known as Akmolinsk before becoming Tselinograd in 1961, and then Akmola in 1992. It is at the junction of the Trans-Kazakhstan and South Siberian railroads, along the banks of the Ishim (Esil) River in the north-central part of the country. The town was originally a Russian military outpost in the 19th century and later became an administrative center for the region. It became particularly important in the 1950s, when the Soviet Union adopted a Virgin Lands policy. There was a tremendous amount of building activity and several research and educational institutions were established in the city. Today there are metal-finishing factories there that process copper, gold, and bauxite from mines in the region. There has been a big population influx into the city even though it is not the biggest city in Kazakhstan. Most of the townspeople work on the railroad and in factories. The population of Astana was 602,480 in 2007.

ALMATY, the former capital of Kazakhstan, has 1.13 million inhabitants. It was named after the apple trees for which it is famous. In 1854 the Russians established a frontier post in Almaty and called it Vernyi. Soon after a fort was established, Cossacks and Siberian peasant farmers settled in the area. The town was devastated by two earthquakes in 1887 and 1911. In 1921, the Soviets changed the name of the town to Alma-ata, meaning "father of apples." In 1929 Alma-ata became the capital of Soviet Kazakhstan. In 1992 the town regained its name of Almaty.

The city is an orderly grid pattern of roads that slope from south to north. It is the financial, cultural, and educational center of the country. Its citizens are service sector workers and industrial workers who work in the tobacco, lumber, and heavy machinery manufacturing industries. Since independence Almaty has developed an air of cosmopolitanism and a spirit of adventure. Many visitors come here in search of opportunities—Chinese Uighur traders from Urumchi, in Xinjiang, sell their wares in the bazaar; foreign experts are eager to advise the government; and Western businesspeople hope to clinch some business deals.

SHYMKENT The city of Shymkent (Chimkent is the Russian spelling) in the south lies along the route of the TurkSib Railroad. It was founded in the 12th century on the strength of trade between the nomads and the citizens of Kokand in Uzbekistan. But this once pretty little town was completely destroyed by heavy Russian shelling in 1864. It has been rebuilt since World War II. Today the main industry is lead smelting from ore mined in the nearby Karatau Hills. The lead is used to make bullets. Shymkent's 545,400 citizens wake up on most days to a pall of gray-brown fumes that hang in the air, a result of pollution caused by the lead smelting industry in the south of the city. There are also chemical works and fruit canneries.

A view of homes in the industrial city of Shymkent.

Architectural monuments, such as these stone figures dating back to the fifth or sixth century, keeps the country's ancient history and culture alive. Previously named Dzhambul, Taraz is also one of the oldest cities in Kazakhstan.

TARAZ is a city that has undergone many name changes. It stands on the site of an old city built in the sixth century. It claims to have been a capital of the Turks in the 11th century, but this distinction is also claimed by the cities of Bukhara in Uzbekistan and Balasagun in Kyrgyzstan. It was an important stop along the Silk Road but was practically destroyed by the Mongols in the 13th century. In 1864 it was captured by the Russians and renamed Aulie-Ata. When Kazakhstan became a republic in 1936, its name was changed again to Zhambyl after a local folk singer Zhambyl Zhabaev. Finally, in 1997, it regained its old name of Taraz. The town has also undergone changes in appearance, from a majestic city of mosques and minarets to one filled with apartment blocks where industry pollutes the air. Three chemical factories produce fertilizer from phosphate ore found in the nearby mountains and pollute the air for the 315,000 people in the city. Taraz and Fresno in California are sister cities, according to Sister Cities International.

SEMEY, 621 miles (1,000 km) north of Almaty, is probably the most Russian-looking of Kazakh towns. It was founded as a Russian fort in 1718 during the reign of Peter the Great and was originally called Semipalatinsk (*palatka* means "tent") because of the tents that were erected around the fort. It became an important trading town in the late 19th century. Its most famous inhabitant was Fyodor Dostoyevsky, a Russian author who was exiled to this place in 1854. Dostoyevsky lived in Semipalatinsk from 1857 to 1859 in a wooden house. Today there is a museum, the F. M. Dostoyevsky Memorial Museum, that includes the house in which he lived. It tells of his life and the time he spent in Semipalatinsk. In more recent years the town was infamous for the secret nuclear testing done nearby in 1949. Fortunately this controversy ended in 1990, but not before statistics showed a higher than average incidence of cancer among its people. Semey, with a population of 330,000, has food-processing, leather, textile, and lumber factories.

The Fyodor Dostoyevsky Memorial Museum in Semey.

HISTORY

A monument in Republic Square
commemorating the heroes who
died in the past wars in Kazakhstan.

CHAPTER 2

HERE HAVE BEEN RECORDS OF human habitation in Kazakhstan since the Stone Age. Petroglyphs, stone monuments, and other cultural artifacts testify to the existence of a nomadic people who tended animals and moved with the seasons because this was the most suitable lifestyle for them.

In the fifth century A.D. the Huns, a nomadic Asian people, under their fierce warrior leader Attila, attacked the great Roman Empire. The Huns were succeeded by tribes of Turkic-speaking people who were organized into political units known as khanates. In the centuries that followed, several regions of Kazakhstan belonged to different empires. During the

Pope Leo I dissuading Attila the Hun from attacking the Roman Empire.

Archaeological evidence has determined that the area that is Kazakhstan today was inhabited as far back as a million years ago. It is one of the centers of Homo sapiens' development and important in the history of ancient humankind.

15th century most of it was part of the Mongol Empire. The Kazakhs, who were in fact Uzbeks who were dissatisfied with their khan, or ruler, did not arrive in Kazakhstan until the 15th century.

GENGHIS KHAN AND THE SILK ROAD

The earliest state that historians are aware of in the region was that of the Turkic Khanate, established in the sixth century A.D. In the eighth century the Kazakhstan region attracted the attention of the outside world because it lay along the Silk Road that connected Europe to China. This route passed near Almaty.

For the next few centuries various parts of the region were dominated by confederations of Turkic tribes and Arabs who introduced Islam to the region. They fought among themselves until Mongol armies invaded the area under the banner of Genghis Khan in the 13th century and imposed Mongol customs on the people.

Genghis Khan (1162-1227) conquered Kazakhstan in the 13th century. The Mongols ruled for two centuries.

A Mongol camp on the move across the desert.

After the Mongol invasion, the tribes in the area came under the control of a succession of khans of the western branch of the Mongol Empire, called the Golden Horde. The Golden Horde later split into smaller groups, including the Nogai Horde and the Uzbek Khanate.

KAZAKHS BREAK AWAY

The Kazakhs emerged as a recognizable group in the mid-15th century, when some of the tribes broke away from the khanates and sought independence.

The breakaway was led by Janybek and Kerey, two sons of the Barak Khan of the White Horde of the Mongol Empire. They led their people in a revolt against Abul Khayr of the Uzbek Khanate. Kazakhs believe this to be the beginning of their nation.

Janybek and Kerey led their supporters to the land near the Chu River. As time went on their supporters and the territory they controlled grew. Although they belonged to the Uzbek tribe, they were also called "Kazakhs" because the word meant a people who had wandered away and who were free and independent. The Kazakhs had a more nomadic lifestyle than the Uzbeks, who were more sedentary.

Their first leader was Khan Kasym, who united the Kazakh tribes. During the late 15th century and throughout the 16th century, the Kazakhs were a strong, nomadic empire that ruled the steppes from the shores of the Caspian and Aral seas in the south and west to the upper Ertis River in the east. Khan Kasym was believed to have in his service more than 200,000 warrior horsemen who were feared by all their neighbors.

An early Kazakh yurt encampment on the grassy steppes of the Ural River.

THREE HORDES EMERGE

This unity, however, was short-lived. During the successive reigns of Khan Kasym's three sons, the Kazakhs soon separated into three new tribal federations called the Great Horde, which controlled the southeastern region north of the Tien Shan Mountains; the Middle Horde, which ruled in the north-central region east of the Aral Sea; and the Lesser Horde, which occupied the west between the Aral Sea and the Ural River. The ruling Khan held the ultimate authority in each horde. But his power was dependent upon that of the sultans, or tribal chiefs, and theirs upon the loyalty of the *biys* (BEES), who were the heads of the clans who made up the horde, and the *batyrs*, who were the warrior class.

This was the situation until the 17th century, when Russian traders and soldiers appeared on the scene. The Russians set up an outpost on the north coast of the Caspian Sea in 1645 and from then on built more forts and seized control of more and more Kazakh territory. In the late 16th and 17th century the Kazakhs were in conflict with Kalmyk invaders of Mongol origin.

From the 1680s to the 1770s the Kazakhs were at war with the Oyrat federation of four western Mongol tribes. The Russians gained increasing control because the Kazakhs were pressured from the east by the Mongols, forcing them westwards. In 1730 Abul Khayr of the Lesser Horde sought Russian help. This alliance unfortunately gave the Russians permanent control over the Lesser Horde. In 1732 part of the Middle Horde was incorporated by Russia, while another part was incorporated by the oath of the Sultan and elders. The Russians conquered the Middle Horde by 1798. The Great Horde managed to remain independent until the 1820s, when the expanding Qugen (Kokend) Khanate in the south forced them to choose Russian protection.

RUSSIANS ESTABLISH A FOOTHOLD

Life on the steppes continued without too much interference from the Russians until the 1820s, when the Russians decided to introduce a new system of administration. The land was divided into administrative units that allowed the Czarist government to tax the people, and Russian military rule was imposed. The three khanates were abolished: the Middle Horde in 1822; the Lesser Horde in 1824; and the Great Horde in 1848.

The Kazakhs resisted Russian rule from the beginning. The first big revolt was led by Khan Kene of the Middle Horde between the years 1837 and 1847. Despite Kazakh resistance, the Russians continued to colonize the land and built a series of forts. Khan Kene was killed in 1847 after a bitter struggle and became the first Kazakh hero. (Khan Kene was also known as Kenesary Kasymov.)

Early Russians in their traditional costumes.

The construction of Russian forts began the destruction of the nomadic life of the people by limiting the area over which the tribes could graze their animals. When Russians settled the fertile lands of northern and eastern Kazakhstan in the 1890s, it signaled the complete destruction of nomadic life there. Then, between 1906 and 1912, more than half a million farms were established by the Russians. As increasing numbers of Russian and Ukrainian peasants arrived, the Kazakhs were forced to emigrate east to China.

When the Russian government tried to recruit the Kazakhs in 1916 to fight against Germany, the people, already starving and displaced from their lands, resisted conscription into the Russian Imperial Army. This resistance, led by Amangeldy Imanov, was brutally crushed. Thousands of Kazakhs were killed, while thousands of others fled to China and Mongolia. As a punishment, those nomads who had taken part in the revolt were driven from their lands, and the area was made available to Russian settlers.

In 1917, when news of the Russian Revolution and the collapse of Imperial Russia reached Kazakhstan, the Kazakhs, led by their Westernized intelligentsia, revolted. Under the leadership of Ali Khan Bukeikhanov, they set up a party called *Alash Orda* (Horde of Alash).

The Bolsheviks took over power in Russia in October 1917 and began to set up revolutionary committees and armed units in Kazakhstan. They allowed the Kazakhs to establish an independent state, called Alash Orda. The Alash Orda survived for two years, from 1918 to 1920, before it was suppressed by the Soviets. The Kazakhs accepted Soviet rule, and some of its leaders became communists. This period of Stalinist terror during the 1920s and the 1930s was also the time when the Kazakh steppes became a part of the infamous Soviet Gulag archipelago. The communists set up camps in this area and deported intellectuals and other dissenters there. Among those who were exiled in Kazakhstan were Soviet literature theoretician Mikhail Bakhtin and writer Alexander Solzhenitsyn.

The years of fighting took its toll on the Kazakhs, who suffered heavy material losses as well as loss of their loved ones.

The Panfilov Park Soviet war memorial in Almaty.

THE SOVIET ERA

In 1936 Kazakhstan became a Soviet republic. During this period the leaders of the republic were mostly non-locals rather than Kazakhs.

From 1929 to 1937 Russian agriculture was collectivized under a policy launched by Soviet leader Joseph Stalin. The Kazakhs suffered because many peasants killed their livestock to protest this policy, and thousands later fled to China and Afghanistan. It is estimated that at least 1.5 million Kazakhs died during this period. In addition the famine killed more than 80 percent of the country's livestock.

War veterans at the Victory Day memorial in Makat in western Kazakhstan.

The Soviets also discouraged nomadic life and encouraged permanent settlement. They pursued an antireligious policy, arresting religious leaders and anyone suspected of being a nationalist. All religious organizations were closed to force people to conform.

To develop the economy, the government promoted industrialization. As industry expanded, skilled workers immigrated to the country. During World War II much of Russia's industry was moved to Kazakhstan to prevent its capture by the Germans.

FORCED RESETTLEMENTS

Various other peoples—Crimean Tatars, Volga Germans, Poles, Chechens, and Koreans—were resettled in the Kazakh region because the Russians distrusted them or were afraid that they would collaborate with Germany during World War II. Other Muslims from neighboring countries, including those from Azerbaijan, and Uighurs from China, also moved to Kazakhstan.

VIRGIN LANDS POLICY

Under Nikita Khrushchev, who was Soviet premier from 1958 to 1964, large areas of virgin or previously uncultivated land in the Ural Mountains, Siberia, and Kazakhstan were opened to farming. The aim was to reduce the import of grain into Central Asia and to encourage the nomadic people to adopt a more settled way of life. Under the program, about 60 percent of Kazakhstan's pastureland was cultivated. Unfortunately there were several things wrong with the program. It was unrealistically based on forecasts of grain production from years of high yield. Thus actual production figures fell short of what was expected. Then there were problems with the climate, soil conditions that were not suited to agriculture; the choice of crop; and the lack of equipment and labor. After several years of crop, failures and other problems, Khrushchev was ousted from his position as premier in 1964.

Leonid Brezhnev died in 1982, when he was still head of the Communist Party.

Between 1953 and 1965 the Soviet campaign to increase the production of wheat and other grains led to large areas of grazing land in the vast grasslands in northern Kazakhstan being put under the plow. This was the Virgin and Idle Lands program. In 1954 Nikita Khrushchev, who was then First Secretary of the Communist Party, sent his assistant Leonid Brezhnev as his representative to Kazakh SSR (Soviet Socialist Republic) to supervise the Virgin and Idle Lands experiment. This program brought another influx of Russian and Ukrainian farmers to the region. After Brezhnev was recalled to Moscow, a Kazakh named Dinmukhamed Kunayev became First Secretary of the Communist Party. However, as a result of the failure of the agricultural policies and other economic problems, Kunayev was forced to resign. He came back into power in 1964 and became the first Kazakh to become a full member of the ruling Politburo of the Soviet Union. As a leader of great foresight and achievement, Kunayev looked after the needs of Kazakhs and Russians with equal care.

FAILED ECONOMY

Kunayev initially raised the standard of living of his people and instituted reforms in higher education that allowed more people to attend college and get better jobs. He stayed in power for over 20 years before coming under attack for mismanagement, favoritism, and misconduct when the economy failed. In 1986 Gorbachev forced him to resign. His dismissal caused unrest—many people took to the streets to demonstrate, producing one of the most serious riots in the Soviet Union in the 1980s.

Kunayev was replaced with an ethnic Russian, Gennadiy Kolbin. Many people were against Kolbin's appointment and rioted and held demonstrations. There are conflicting reports a s to how many people were killed, injured, and arrested in this unrest. Some reports say at least 200 people died and more than 1,000 were injured. Kolbin was an administrator who instituted economic and social reforms that were Soviet-inspired and unrealistic, causing the economy to deteriorate further. Agricultural output continued to drop so low in 1989 that Kolbin suggested killing wild ducks that were migrating through the country to provide meat for the people.

Mikhail Gorbachev was president of the Soviet Union from 1985 to 1991.

RISE OF NATIONALISM

Starting in 1989 conflicts developed in the Soviet Union between the central parliament of the USSR and the parliaments of the individual republics, mainly over the respective powers that each should have. There were increasing demands in the republics for autonomy and even for full independence. At the Congress of People's Deputies in Moscow in June 1989 many informal political groups presented their nationalist programs. This feeling of nationalism was also echoed in Kazakhstan.

In June 1989 Kolbin returned to Moscow and was replaced by Nursultan Nazarbayev. In March 1990 elections were held. A new legislature consisting of a majority of ethnic Kazakhs and a minority of Russians was formed.

NAZARBAYEV IN POWER

Nazarbayev, a Kazakh, trained as a metallurgist and an engineer, proved himself to be a skilled politician. He became a member of the Communist Party in 1979 and was made chairman of Kazakhstan's Council of Ministers in 1984. When Kunayev fell out of favor, Nazarbayev took a major role in the attacks against Kunayev. Although he was passed over in favor of Kolbin in 1986, Nazarbayev was a strong supporter of Gorbachev and his reform programs. He realized the importance of balancing Moscow's demands with increasing Kazakh nationalism. After he took over, he made Kazakh the official language, allowed for greater religious tolerance, and permitted criticism and an examination of the negative effects that collectivization and other Soviet policies had on the country.

Nursultan Nazarbayev swearing the oath as president in 1999.

The late 1980s was a time of tremendous turmoil in the Soviet Union, which was facing imminent breakup. Gorbachev attempted to hold the union together by calling for the election of a national legislature and a loosening of Soviet political control over the republics.

Throughout the times, Nazarbayev supported Gorbachev and the Soviet Union because he believed that the member republics were too economically dependent on each other to be able to survive on their own. But he was also aware of the importance of gaining control of the country's mineral wealth. In June 1991, at his insistence, Moscow surrendered control of the mineral resources in Kazakhstan.

In September 1991 the three republics of Estonia, Latvia, and Lithuania achieved complete independence and were recognized as sovereign states. Several other republics were demanding independence. Gorbachev tried to establish a new "union of sovereign states" that would have some common foreign, defense, and economic policies, but no agreement could be reached with the remaining republics.

On December 16, 1991, Kazakhstan declared independence. On December 21, 1991, 11 of the 15 republics, including Kazakhstan, signed documents for the dissolution of the Soviet Union and the establishment of the Commonwealth of Independent States (CIS) that would share a common policy for foreign affairs and defense.

Nazarbayev, who has remained in power until today, has steered a careful course for his country. Kazakhstan is still heavily dependent upon Russia, and is in the CIS, which is strongly influenced by Russia. At the same time Nazarbayev tries to balance this by cultivating relations with China, Kazakhstan's Central Asian neighbors, and the West.

An independence monument shows a golden warrior standing on the back of a snow leopard.

GOVERNMENT

The presidential palace of
Kazakhstan in Astana City.

FOR MORE THAN TWO CENTURIES Kazakhstan was under Russian control, first imperial czarist rule, then communist Soviet rule. When independence was declared on December 16, 1991, Nursultan Nazarbayev became the country's first president, and Kazakhstan retained the basic government structure and most of the leaders who were in power under the Soviets.

The current president, Nursultan Nazarbayev, has been in power for more than 20 years. Although observers of the political situation in Kazakhstan believe that there has not been a free and fair election in the country, Nazarbayev has presided over his country's rise from the ruins of Soviet occupation and is popular with his people.

A patriotic poster with the national flags of Kazakhstan flying behind it.

CONSTITUTIONS OF 1993 AND 1995

The post-independence government of Kazakhstan consists of: the president, who is the head of government; an executive branch, represented by the council of ministers; a legislative branch that is the parliament; and the judicial branch.

Two new constitutions, written in 1993 and 1995, have ensured the power of the president and his control over various aspects of the government.

The 1993 constitution replaced the Soviet constitution, in force since 1978. Under this constitution the prime minister and the Council of Ministers are responsible only to the president. A new constitution in 1995 reinforced this relationship and placed the country under direct presidential rule. The constitution was drawn up by President Nazarbayev and his council of ministers. It was adopted by popular referendum on August 30, 1995. This constitution also guarantees equal rights to people of all nationalities and made Kazakh and Russian the official state languages.

President Nazarbayev looks on as his wife, Sara, casts her vote during the 2005 elections.

Under the constitution the president is the head of state. He is elected for a maximum of two consecutive, five-year terms. He governs with the help of the council of ministers, whose key members he appoints. The head of the council is the prime minister. The president appoints the prime minister and other ministers of the council, as well as the chairperson of the National Security Committee. The president also has the authority to issue decrees and overrule actions taken by the ministries.

TWO HOUSES OF PARLIAMENT

Parliament, as established by the 1995 constitution, is made up of two houses, the Senate and the Assembly or Mazhilis. There are 47 seats in the Senate; 7 senators are appointed by the president. There are 77 members of the Mazhilis who are selected by popular election. Members of the Senate serve a six-year term while those in the Mazhilis remain in office for five years.

A person wishing to run for the Senate must be a citizen for at least 5 years, 30 years or older, have higher education, and have lived in the territory he or she wishes to represent for not less than 3 years. A member of the Mazhilis must be a citizen and at least 25 years old. All Kazakh citizens 18 years and above are eligible to vote.

Members of the Senate and Mazhilis deal with the making of laws and their reform, the economy and the budget, international affairs, defense and security, regional development, and local administration.

The parliament building in Alma Ata.

The country is divided into 14 provinces, plus two cities—Almaty, the former capital, and Astana, the current capital—as well as the territory of Baykonur (formerly called Leninsk). Almaty, Astana, and Baykonur have a special administrative status that is equal to a province. Each province is subdivided into regions and smaller administrative units of settlements. Every province has its own council responsible for budget, tax, and other administrative matters.

The heads of local administration, known as akim (a-keem), are appointed by the president and can only be removed from office by a two-thirds majority vote of no confidence by the local councils.

ACTIVE POLITICAL CLIMATE

Although the president has not encouraged a democratic society, he has balanced his authoritarian rule with allowance for opposition. However, opposition parties are not major players in the Kazakhstan Parliament.

The political change that Kazakhstan has undergone since independence has led to a proliferation of social organizations, political parties, and special interest groups. There are 11 officially registered political parties that have formed, reformed, split, and combined. Some special interest groups include the Russian Cossacks, Pensioners Movement, and Peasant Union. Political groups include the Legal Development of Kazakhstan, the Independent Miners Union, and several human rights groups.

THE JUDICIAL BRANCH

Justice is served in Kazakhstan by the Supreme Court and local courts of the country. Small local courts hear cases of petty crime, such as vandalism, while provincial courts deal with bigger crimes, such as murders. Cases of appeal are sent to the Supreme Court. The judicial branch also includes a Constitutional Council made up of seven members who serve six-year terms of office. Ex-presidents of the country are life members of the

The Assembly of the Peoples of Kazakhstan is also a consultative and advisory body under the president. Its tasks include the promotion and maintenance of ethnic and social stability. It makes policies and finds solutions for any social and cultural conflicts in Kazakh society. The establishment of the Assembly in 1995 indicates the importance that President Nazarbayev has given to the balance of multilateral ethnic interests, and to conflicts between Kazakh nationalist interests and Slavic insecurities. The president, who is chairman of the Assembly, convenes the Assembly at his own initiative or when asked to do so by at least a third of the assembly members. The members are made up of candidates sent by smaller assemblies in each region of the country.

Constitutional Council. Today there are 44 judges in the Supreme Court, all appointed by the president.

The Ministry of Justice building.

Of the seven Constitutional Council judges, two are nominated by the president, two by the chairman of the Senate, and two by the chairman of the *Mazhilis*. The chairman of the council is appointed by the president and is very powerful because he has the deciding vote if the council members are deadlocked over a case. The council members serve for six years. Half the members are appointed every three years. The 1995 constitution makes all former presidents of the republic automatic members of the council for life.

Council members may not be members of parliament, nor can they hold other employment except for some teaching, scientific, or creative activity. They may not be engaged in any private business or sit on an advisory council of a commercial enterprise.

It is the responsibility of the Constitutional Council to settle disputes about presidential and general elections, as well as those among parliamentary deputies. Besides ensuring that the laws to be adopted conform to the constitution, the council has to interpret the constitution and resolve all matters regarding constitutional procedures.

From left to right, Kyrgyz president Askar Akayev, Kazakhstan president Nursultan Nazarbayev, Tajik president Emomali Rakhmonov, Russian president Vladimir Putin, and Uzbek president Islam Karimov meet during the Central Asian Cooperation summit.

Besides the Constitutional Council there are a number of advisory bodies under the direct control of the president. These are the Security Council, concerned with matters of defense and national security; the High Court Council; the National Council for State (National) Policy; and special committees dealing with mass media, and issues of human rights, family, and women.

SMALL ARMY

When Kazakhstan became independent in 1991 it had no military force because its defense and security matters had been taken care of by the Soviet army. A Kazakh military force was established in 1992 when the former Soviet 40th Army, stationed on Kazakh soil, was nationalized. Kazakhstan now has a general-purpose army, border troops, a small air force, and a navy for patrolling the Caspian Sea. But it continues to be dependent on Russia. In 1995 the two countries signed an agreement, and Russian troops now join Kazakhs in patrolling the country's borders.

RELATIONS WITH NEIGHBORS

Despite the breakup of the Soviet Union Kazakhstan's ties with the former members of the union are still strong, and there are bilateral trade and

THE COUNTRY'S LEADERS

President Nursultan Narzabayev has been in the highest position of leadership since the country's independence from the Soviet Union in 1991. He brought to this job his credentials as chairman of the council of ministers and his experience as First Secretary of the Kazakh Communist Party. The 1993 constitution strengthened the position of the executive, and thus Narzabayev's position, in the government. This was reinforced by the 1995 constitution and a referendum that extended his term of office until 2000. He was re-elected in 1999 and 2005. In 2007 a constitutional amendment was approved by Parliament that would allow President Nazarbayev to seek unlimited re-election to office. A number of opposition parties have objected to what they see as the president's undisguised attempts to entrench himself in power.

The prime minister is Karim K. Massimov, an economist by training, who received his education from universities in Beijing and Wuhan, China. He has been prime minister of Kazakhstan since 2007.

The first deputy prime minister is Umirzak Shukeev, an economist educated in Moscow. He has been government advisor in economic affairs, governor of Kostanai Oblast and South Kazakhstan Oblast, and mayor of Astana. He has held the post of prime minister since 2007.

security agreements with these countries. In 1994 Kazakhstan, Uzbekistan, and Kyrgyzstan set up a free-trade zone. Kazakhstan also tries to play a part in maintaining peace in the region. With Russia and Uzbekistan, it has tried to mediate in the civil war in Tajikistan.

Kazakhstan's relationship with China has been a careful one. The Chinese are next-door neighbors, and Kazakhstan has always been wary of the possibility of Chinese domination. There are many Kazakhs living across the border in China, and since independence many Chinese have bought property in Kazakhstan and are living there. There is also a lot of trade between the two countries, as well as direct road and rail links.

Kakakhstan has received some financial aid from Iran in developing transportation links, Oman in building oil pipeline, Egypt in building mosques, and Israel in agriculture.

ECONOMY

A modern office building in Astana city.

CHAPTER 4

K AZAKHSTAN HAS ENORMOUS
reserves of fossil fuel, minerals, coal,
and metals—iron ore, manganese,
nickel, cobalt, copper, molybdenum, lead,
zinc, bauxite, gold, uranium, phosphate,
and silver. Mining is therefore an important
industry. However, there is also a large
agricultural sector.

For most of its modern history Kazakhstan's economy was closely tied
to that of the Soviet Union. Its mineral resources were tapped and sent
north to meet the production needs of Russian industry, which was
developed to fulfill the demands of the Soviet consumer. Independence
meant that Kazakhstan had to completely take charge of its economy
and revamp its entire economic infrastructure. It is trying to reduce its
dependence on the export of its natural resources by balancing this with
a developing manufacturing industry.

The Karachaganak-Uralsk natural gas pipeline.

RICH RESERVES

Of all its natural resources, oil is at present the country's most productive and lucrative. The oil reserves, found mainly in the northern end of the Caspian Sea, have been estimated to be as much as 30 billion barrels, according to sources in the industry. Most of this is in new fields that have not yet been exploited.

The country's main oil reserves lie in the western part. There are currently three major oil fields: Tengiz, Uzen, and Karachaganak. Unfortunately Kazakhhstan's oil and gas industry has traditionally depended on the Russian demand for crude oil. Since the breakup of the Soviet Union there has been a drop in production at Russian refineries. This has affected production levels in Kazakhstan, although most of its oil is still exported to Russia.

Another problem for Kazakhstan in expanding the export of oil is that, to reach Western customers, it has to rely on pipeline access through Russia. In the mid-1990s the only way to export oil was through a northbound pipeline linking Atyrau in northwestern Kazakhstan with Samara in Russia. In 2001 a Caspian Pipeline Consortium pipeline connected Kazakh oil fields with the

The Atyrau refinery is a subsidiary of Kazakhstan's state-owned oil and gas company, KazMunaiGaz.

The race is on to see who can benefit from the rich oil deposits in the Caspian Sea area. Kazakhstan and its neighbors, Azerbaijan and Turkmenistan, have enormous energy resources that, until the breakup of the Soviet Union, were exported from the region through Russian pipelines. Pipeline connections between the Tengiz oilfield and the Russian port of Novorossiysk are being improved by a group of international companies. China and Kazakhstan are constructing a pipeline from Kazakhstan to the west of China. Other possible routes include moving the oil through Iran and Afghanistan. As U.S. Energy Secretary Federico Pena said in November 1997 at a Caspian Pipeline conference, "We are building a new Silk Road, but the commodities now are not silk and spices, they are oil and gas. The paths will be taken not by camels and caravans, but by pipelines, fiber optics, and railroads."

Russian Black Sea port of Novorossiysk. A more recent Kazakhstan-China oil pipeline runs from the Caspian shore to Xinjiang in China.

Despite its enormous fuel reserves Kazakhstan has to import oil and gas, because an undeveloped transportation network between the eastern and western parts of the country makes it difficult to use its own resources for industrial development. Kazakhstan has no pipelines to transport oil from the resource-rich west to the populated east.

Oil, natural gas, and other fuels are imported from Russia. Oil from the western oil fields is sent across the border to refineries in Russia, while Russian oil from Siberia feeds the refineries in eastern Kazakhstan.

Kazakhstan has enormous reserves of natural gas, especially in the northwest near the Russian border. The country also has three major coal fields in Torghay, Karaganda, and Ekibastuz. Much of the coal is used in thermoelectric stations to produce power and to produce steel. Kazakhstan exports coal to Russia and to the other CIS states.

Phosphate, iron ore, manganese, chromite, lead, zinc, copper, titanium, bauxite, silver, phosphates, and cobalt are mined. Since independence, other foreign countries have shown interest in developing these resources with the Kazakh government.

Men standing on top of a cotton harvest in Turkestan. Cotton is one of Kazakhstan's major crops. The vast country has enormous agricultural potential with its rich steppe lands.

INDUSTRY

Before 1991 Kazakhstan had a large manufacturing and processing industry. Following independence, industrial production remained the most important sector of the economy. There is a machine-building industry specializing in manufacturing construction equipment, tractors, bulldozers, agricultural machines, and military defense equipment. Metallurgy, or the processing of metals, and the production of chemicals, petrochemicals, and construction materials are also important. Light industries include the canning of fruit and vegetables, milling, brewing, and wine-making.

AGRICULTURE

Agriculture is the second-most important segment of the economy after industry. The main agricultural regions are the north-central and southern parts of the country. Growing grain, especially wheat, is the main activity in the north-central region, while cotton and rice are the main crops in the south. Kazakhstan also produces meat, wool, and milk. Much of the agricultural land is under the control of the government. Farms are usually jointly owned state and collective farms or belong to farming associations.

The climate and soil is most suited to the grazing of animals, thus the traditional Kazakh nomadic lifestyle, where people follow their herds of sheep, cattle, camels, and horses as they graze on the open steppes. Nomadic life was disrupted when Soviet policy in the 1950s and 1960s introduced widespread cultivation of the land.

WORKFORCE

In the past most workers were employed in state enterprises, and before independence, women made up about half of the total number of workers. This high participation of women workers meant that about 80 percent of the population of working age was employed. But these high employment figures may not have been accurate because, until independence, it was Soviet policy not to acknowledge unemployment. Russians tended to have higher-paying, skilled jobs in sectors such as transportation, industry, and science, while Kazakhs predominated in the lower-paid jobs.

Since independence large numbers of skilled managers and technicians, mainly of Russian or Slav descent, have moved out of the country, and for a while this affected the growth of the economy. But Kazakhs quickly learned to fill in the gaps.

The labor force of Kazakhstan is almost 9 million, mostly employed in industry and manufacturing and in agriculture and forestry. The remaining workforce can be found in the construction, transportation, communications, trade, and service industries.

> ## TENGE
>
> *The tenge was introduced in 1993 to replace the Soviet ruble. The word* tenge *in Kazakh means a set of scales, bringing in the idea of balance and equality. November 15, the day that the new national currency was introduced, is celebrated as the "Day of National Currency of the Republic of Kazakhstan." One tenge equals 100 tijn.*

Today the country's workforce is estimated to be about 9 million strong. There is a drive by the government to see that Kazakhs are well educated and able to participate in a higher level of services and industry and new technologies.

BANKING

Since 1993 the Kazakh banking system has been organized into two levels. At the top is the National Bank of Kazakhstan, which regulates the country's banking system and ensures that the national currency, the tenge, is strong and stable. All other commercial banks, whether private or owned by the state, comprise the second level.

The period immediately following independence was a time of great stress for the economy. Government price controls were removed, the rate of inflation rose, and the price of food, services, and other products got so high that the people's buying power was greatly reduced. There

Nurbank is another trading company in Almaty.

was a banking boom and more than 200 small banks opened for business. However, the National Bank took control of the situation and strengthened banking laws and stabilized the monetary system. In 2001 there were fewer than 50 banks operating.

TRADE AND FOREIGN INVESTMENT

Before independence Kazakhstan traded mainly with the Russian Federation. Today Russia continues to be Kazakhstan's biggest import and export partner, but the government is working hard to open the country up to international trade by stabilizing the economy, deregulating, and liberalizing trade regulations. Its major CIS trading partners are Kyrgyzstan, Uzbekistan, Belarus, and the Ukraine, all of which import more from Kazakhstan than they export to it. Other important trading partners include China, Italy, Germany, Switzerland, the Czech Republic, and the Netherlands. Kazakhstan imports more from the United States than it exports to the country.

The country's stable government and abundant natural resources have made Kazakhstan an attractive place for foreign investment. Companies from Great Britain, the United States, and France have all registered their interest in investing in the country. There is a growing middle class of citizens who are eager to join foreign companies in taking advantage of the opportunities created by the increasing economic openness of the country. Foreign investment is important in the development of important sectors of Kazakh industry, especially in the oil and gas, mining, and construction sectors.

Cranes at the cargo port of Pavlodar. Kazakhstan exports mostly raw materials (ferrous and nonferrous metals, oil and petroleum products, and chemicals) and imports mostly manufactured goods (machinery, food, equipment, vehicles, and chemicals).

Sending satellites into space is one of the more unusual ways Kazakhstan earns foreign exchange. It can put a satellite into orbit for any country at a lower cost than that charged by the U.S. National Aeronautics and Space Administration (NASA). Although the space facility is called Baykonur Cosmodrome, it is closer to the town of Leninsk; the town of Baykonur is 186 miles (299 km) north. The launch site used to be guarded with secrecy, but it has been open to the public since 1991 under certain conditions. The complex is a bewildering network of launch pads, gantries, and tracking stations. Launches literally shake the earth. The Cosmodrome is funded and managed by the Russians.

IMPROVING AIR, ROAD, AND RAIL LINKS

Independent Kazakhstan inherited the poor telecommunications and transportation networks from its Soviet days. This was due to the generally inhospitable land that lay between populated areas. Only the largest cities are linked by both road and rail. Communication lines tend to run north to south, as Kazakhstan has traditionally looked north to Russia. Most freight is carried by rail, while people travel by road.

Almaty and Astana have the two biggest and busiest airports with connecting flights to Russia, member countries of the CIS, China. After independence Kazakhstan Airlines was set up with 100 aircraft, part of the USSR's fleet that was divided among the former Soviet republics. It has since stopped operating. The country's national airline is now Air Astana, formed in 2001 by the government and a British aerospace company. Several private airline companies also operate in Kazakhstan, including the airlines of the Ukraine and Uzbekistan, Lufthansa of Germany, British Airways, Turkish, Iranian and Russian airlines.

A view of the airport terminal in Astana.

Kazakhstan has good road and rail links with Russia, China, and other Central Asian states. The Kazakh (formerly Turkistan-Siberian) Railway, built with forced labor in the 1930s, links Kazakhstan with the Trans-Siberian Railway. The Urumchi-Almaty line was completed in 1990, linking Kazakhstan with Xinjiang in China via a border crossing at Druzhba (the name is Russian for "friendship"). There is also a border crossing by road to Xinjiang at Khorgos, 25 miles (40 km) from the Kazakh town of Panfilov.

Although Kazakhstan is landlocked, it has two inland river waterways—the Syr Darya River in the south-central region and the Ertis River in the north. They are used to transport freight and passengers.

Kazakhstan's old and inadequate telecommunications facilities that existed before independence have received much developmental attention. In 1994 only 17 out of 100 people in the cities and fewer than 8 out of every 100 in the rural areas had telephones. Telephone lines would break down frequently, and spare parts were hard to get because much of the equipment came from the Soviet Union and Eastern Europe and was obsolete. Today telecommunications is a leading sector of the economy and attracts foreign investment. Kazakhtelekom, a national company, provides local and international telecommunications services. Trunk lines are being developed, and Internet and mobile services are increasing. Kazakhstan is well connected on the Internet. There are a number of Internet servers, and many websites, commercial and state-owned, offer a wealth of information about the country.

ENVIRONMENT

Sunflowers growing in the richly fertile grasslands of the Altai Mountains.

CHAPTER 5

AZAKHSTAN'S ENVIRONMENTAL concerns are in many ways similar to those faced by many nations: the impact of agriculture on the land, the need to produce enough crops to support its population, pollution from industrialization and the extraction of natural resources, and increasing urbanization.

In addition Kazakhstan has problems that are unique to its situation— the Virgin Lands policy of Soviet period and the decades of nuclear testing that took place from the 1950s onward.

The big Almaty Lake, located in the Zailijskiy Ala Tau mountains in Ili Alatay National Park, is 8,235 feet (2,510 m) above sea level.

Grain crops being harvested at a collective farm in the Taldu Kurgansk Region of Kazakhstan. Many parcels of land were cleared in Kazakhstan to make room for the agricultural boom.

Kazakhstan is a beautiful land, uniquely situated in the center of the Asian continent. The climate is difficult and the land fragile. It has hundreds of species of flora and fauna, many not found anywhere else in the world.

POLLUTION

AGRICULTURAL POLLUTION Land use continues to be quite traditional. More than 80 percent of the land is under agricultural use, much of it is for pasturing animals. The environmental problems facing Kazakhstan are natural as well as man made. People living in the river valleys and fertile areas around the rivers have a tremendous impact on the country's fragile water ecosystems. Agriculture puts a strain on water resources through over-demand for water, need for irrigation, and pollution.

INDUSTRIAL POLLUTION Bad urban planning and industrialization have created additional problems of pollution. The mining industry has indiscriminately dumped tailings, ash, rubble, and other waste products on the land. Kazakhstan is fortunate to have enormous reserves of oil, but the extraction of these resources has also been environmentally detrimental. It has transformed large areas of land from the pristine, natural state or lower-impact agricultural use. Oil production requires a tremendous infrastructure—thousands of miles of pipeline, roads, oil wells, and support buildings have to be constructed.

Extracting oil is an environmentally risky business. The risks are not unique to Kazakhstan. Wherever oil is being taken from the ground, it disrupts the natural environment, be it fragile steppe land, rain forest, or an ocean habitat. We only have to remember the 2010 Gulf of Mexico oil disaster to realize the truth of this statement.

AIR POLLUTION, particular in the cities and industrial centers, is high. The main polluting industries are ferrous and nonferrous metallurgy, the production of heat and energy, chemical and oil processing, and mineral fertilizer production. Plants in industrial areas emit pollutants and effluent with very little control. Many cities such as Almaty, Shymkent, Taraz, Ekibastuz, and Pavlodar have many times the maximum admissible concentration of pollutants such as sulfur dioxide, benzapyrene, zinc, chrome, lead, iron, chlorine, and mercury, just to name a few. The increasing number of automobiles releasing gases into the atmosphere is adding to the problem. As a result many people become ill or die from cardiovascular diseases. Apart from air pollution, the people who live in these cities suffer from other forms of pollution such as noise, vibration, electrical magnetic fields, and other physical factors.

Polluted smoke coming from a steel factory in Karaghandy.

Rivers and lakes such as the White Berel River in the Altai Mountains would have been in danger of pollution, had conservationists not stepped in.

EFFECTS OF POLLUTION

In most countries agriculture, industry, and urbanization are the main sources of environmental concern. But in Kazakhstan there is an additional, unique environmental concern resulting from nuclear testing and rocket launching. The sites associated with former defense industries and test ranges are radioactive and chemically toxic. They pose a severe health risk to people and animals.

All these problems are compounded by the fact that Kazakhstan also has a very fragile natural environment. According to the Ministry of Environment Protection, large areas in the Taldykorgan, South Kazakhstan, and Kyzylorda oblasts are vulnerable to wind erosion. Soil erosion due to water runoff is a problem in the south Kazakhstan, Almaty, and Aktubinsk oblasts. Much of the country's water supply has been polluted by industrial and agricultural runoff.

Chemical contamination of the water has killed and made life difficult for the flora and fauna that depend upon this ecosystem, from the smallest living organisms such as bacteria and algae to the fish, plants, and animals that thrive on them. The two main rivers that flowed into the Aral Sea have been diverted for irrigation. The sea is drying up and leaving behind a layer of chemical pesticides and natural salts. These substances are then picked up by the wind.

CARING FOR WHAT IS NATURALLY THERE

The Ministry of Environment Protection is the department that works with United Nations (UN) agencies, nongovernmental organizations, community groups, and individuals to redress environmental problems and to see that protective legislation is in place. The ministry has identified a number of important and distinctively different ecological systems in Kazakhstan. These are the high-altitude mountain ecological system, the forest steppes, the grass steppes, the desert areas, and the wetlands.

There are four large mountainous regions mostly in the western part of the country—the Western Tien Shan, Northern Tien Shan, Kazakhstan-Dzhungar, and Altai ranges. Although these are relatively inaccessible areas because of altitude, nevertheless these areas have been much altered and disturbed by agriculture, forestry, recreational needs, and the construction of roads and cities.

The forest steppes are in the north, covering the region of the cities of Petropavlovsk and Kokshetau. Although this is a small region overall, these steppes are an important ecological anchor because they are rich in various types of grass and they protect the soils of the adjacent steppe lands.

The Kazakhstan steppe is the ecological zone that has been most transformed by human activity. There was wide-scale plowing and opening up of the land to agriculture, especially during the Virgin Land period from 1954 to 1960. This destroyed much of the natural grasses and in their place weeds have been introduced into these acres that were made arable.

In the desert areas the worst destruction of plant cover has occurred in the foothill zones where the land was used for the pasturing of animals and trees were cut for fuel. This has caused soil erosion and increasing desertification, making areas that were once agriculturally productive into infertile land.

There are more than 100 different species of fish in the lakes and rivers of Kazakhstan. Many of these are important to the fishing industry. They include several varieties of sturgeon, sprat, pike, roach, bream, and perch. Since 1978 the government has published a Red Data Book that keeps a record of the diversity of flora and fauna and their status as disappeared, endangered, or stable.

A citrine wagtail searching for food on the shores of the wetlands in the Korgalzhyn State Nature Reserve. The natural landscape of Kazakhstan is home to many different species of birds.

MARINE LIFE

Kazakhstan's wet and marshy areas lie in the north. Here thousands of lakes are important nesting areas for local sandpipers, seagulls, terns, and other waterfowl. Being situated in the center of the Asian continent, this area is also a crucial nesting and resting site for many bird species migrating from Siberia to the Caspian Sea and from Asia and Africa.

CONSERVATION EFFORTS

The government is aware that it has to balance the need to develop the land and use its resources for the country's economic growth with the necessity of preserving the unique heritage of Kazakhstan's natural wealth. It has established many national parks and nature and game reserves. These reserves preserve special ecosystems such as the mountains, desert, lakes, forests, and the vast steppes. These areas are under the protection of the Ministry of Natural Resources and Ministry of Environmental Protection.

Kazakhstan has signed a number of international environmental agreements, such as the UN Convention on Biological Diversity, the UN Conference on Environment and Development (Rio-92) and the Kyoto Forum on Climate Change. In a number of areas it has to work act with its neighbors to protect natural resources that these various countries share. For instance Kazakhstan, Uzbekistan, and Kyrgyzstan are committed to the conservation of the West Tien-Shan Biodiversity.

ARAL SEA ENVIRONMENTAL DISASTER

Kazakhstan shares the Aral Sea with neighboring Uzbekistan. In ancient times this sea was a fertile and rich area, providing a livelihood for the traders, hunters, and fishing people who lived here. The word aral *in Kazakh means "island." This was a reference to the more than one thousand islands that dotted these waters.*

The Aral Sea was an important stopping point along the Silk Road linking Europe and Asia. Once it was the fourth-largest lake in the world. Today the sea is very much reduced in size. It has shrunk so much that it is now composed of three smaller, separate bodies of water—the North Aral Sea and the eastern and western basins of the South Aral Sea. This is because the two rivers, the Amu Darya and the Syr Darya, that feed into the Aral Sea have been diverted for irrigating the agricultural lands. It was part of the Soviet plan to regenerate the surrounding desert for the growing of crops.

As the lake dried up it increased in salinity to such an extent that it is now toxic for the fish and wildlife that used to depend upon it. Thousands of people who used to fish here have abandoned their livelihood. One can see abandoned fishing boats and other disused equipment littering the dry and dusty Aral shores. The winds that blow across the land pick up the salt and dust and carry it miles away. The dust carries an unhealthy amount of chemicals from pesticides and fertilizers.

This creates a health problem for the people who suffer from an increase in cardiovascular, cancer, tubercular, and respiratory diseases. Kazakhstan; its neighbors Uzbekistan, Tajikistan, Turkmenistan, and Kyrgyzstan; and international organizations are trying to reverse the Aral Sea tragedy, which has been described as one of the world's worst environmental disasters. These efforts include the creation of dams to help fill the sea, improving the quality of irrigation canals, moving away from water-intensive crops, and redirecting water from other rivers into the sea. In the recent years there was a relatively successful effort by Kazakhstan to refill the North Aral with water by building a dam.

The beautiful sand dune formation in the Altyn-Emel reserve in Almaty.

NATURE RESERVES

The Aksu-Zhabagly nature reserve in South Kazakhstan, set up in 1927, at the foot of the West Tien Shan mountains, is the oldest established nature reserve in Kazakhstan and probably all of Central Asia. It covers more than 210,039 acres (85,000 hectares). Here can be found thousands of plant species, more than 200 bird species, and almost 50 different species of animals. It is home to the Siberian ibex, Roe and Caspian deer, boars, weasels, and vultures. Among the rare animals in this reserve are the snow leopard, the Turkestan lynx, the Pamir argali, the red bear, the golden eagle (Kazakhstan's national bird), the Saker falcon, and the short-toed eagle. The Karabastau and Akbastau paleontological sites on the slopes of Karatau Mountain have fossils of fish, mollusks, tortoises, and insects from the Jurassic period, because this area was once under the sea.

The Nauryzym nature reserve, covering more than 214,981 acres (87,000 ha) in the Kostanai region, is the second-oldest reserve in Kazakhstan. It was set up primarily to preserve the Nauryzym pine forest. However, the wetlands of the reserve are also an important habitat for numerous bird species, many of them endangered. The white heron is one of the rare and interesting inhabitants of the reserve.

In the 1960s and later Kazakhstan established many more reserves, among them the Kurgaldzhino, Almaty, Markakol, Ustyurt, and West-Altai reserves. Kurgaldzhino in the Akmola region is the sanctuary of the pink flamingo, whose nests in Lake Tengiz are the most northernmost of its species in the world. In addition the Tengiz-Kurgaldzhino lakes attract migratory waterfowl and other birds such as the Dalmatian pelican and

NUCLEAR TESTING IN KAZAKHSTAN

The Semipalatinsk test site was the main testing area for nuclear weapons during the country's Soviet days. It is on the steppes of the northeastern corner of the country, south of the valley of the Irtysh River. The site was established in 1947 and operated until it was closed in 1991. The town of Semipalatinsk was later renamed Semey.

The first test, called Operation First Lightning, was conducted in 1949. It scattered radioactive fallout on the nearby villages, some of which were not evacuated. During its period of operation, more than 500 nuclear experiments were carried out on or above ground. The cumulative impact of these experiments has been likened to several thousand times the impact of the atomic bomb that fell on Hiroshima, Japan, during World War II.

This caused tremendous environmental pollution in the areas affected by the fallout and injured thousands of people over at least three generations who were exposed to the radiation. There have been birth defects and mutations and high incidences of cancer, immunological deficiencies, and other diseases among the population in the area. Kazakhstan is now in the forefront of global efforts to fight for nuclear disarmament. President Nazarbayev has written a book, entitled The Epicenter of Peace, *devoted to this cause.*

mute swan. This swampy, marshy reserve has been designated a protected landscape by the United Nations Educational, Scientific, and Cultural Organization (UNESCO).

The Altyn-Emel reserve in Almaty oblast, founded in 1961, is especially known for a natural phenomenon called sand barkhans. These crescent-shaped sand dunes are called "singing sands" for the loud sounds they produce when the wind blows over them or when one walks on them. A similar phenomenon can be found in California's Kelso Dunes and Eureka Dunes and the Warren Dunes of southwestern Michigan.

KAZAKHS

Kazakh children doing their homework in a small mountain village along the old Silk Road of Kazakhstan.

>THERE ARE ABOUT 15,460,484 (2010 estimate) people living in Kazakhstan, but it is only since independence that indigenous Kazakhs have regained the majority in their own country. When Kazakhstan was part of the Soviet Union, Russians, Ukrainians, and Belorussians formed more than half the population.

A modern Kazakh family at the Bayterek building in Astana.

A Kazakh family of Turkish origin.

Since 1991 many of them have returned to their homeland. At the same time many Kazakhs from other parts of the world have returned to Kazakhstan.

Traditionally Kazakh men wear a *chapan*, a wraparound robe made of cotton or wool and fastened with a belt at the waist. It looks like a dressing gown. The women wear colorful, sleeveless velvet jackets that are often ornately embroidered. The men wear caps on their heads and the women head scarves. Today it is common to see Kazakhs in modern dress, and traditional clothing is not common.

The Kazakhs emerged as a separate and recognizable group sometime in the middle of the 15th century. Their ancestors were nomadic people who were a mixture of Turkic tribes who lived in the area for centuries. Turkic people are descended from the Turks who, according to historians, were the first people to speak a Turkic language. A very powerful Turk Empire ruled Central Asia in the first century A.D. Although it was a short-lived empire, the Turks left behind a long-lasting legacy and left their mark on all the people of Central Asia.

After the Turks came a long line of different empires. There were the Uighurs, the Kyrgyz, the Khitans, the Mongols, and the Uzbeks. Both the modern Uzbeks and Kazakhs were formed from a blurred ancestry of the overlapping tribes and peoples of Central Asia.

HORDES

Historically Kazakhs can be divided into three clans or hordes. Each clan has its own territory. Kazakhs of the Lesser Horde come from western Kazakhstan, between the Aral Sea and the Ural River; the Middle Horde dominate the northern and central part of Kazakhstan east of the Aral Sea; the Great Horde belong to the southeastern area north of the Tien Shan Mountains.

Kazakhs of the Lesser and Middle Hordes were the first to come under Russian domination and tend to be more Russified. Many of their children were sent to study in Russian schools. Early Kazakh nationalists were often from these Lesser and Middle Hordes. They involved themselves in politics even before the Russian Revolution and were the targets of Stalin's purges during the 1930s when he tried to get rid of the Kazakh intelligentsia.

The Great Horde Kazakhs were the last to come under Russian control because, being in the south, they were farthest away from Russia. They were politicized only after the revolution. But members of the Great Horde have dominated Kazakh politics. This was especially evident when the capital of the country was moved to Almaty in the south. Both presidents, Dinmukhamed Kunayev and Nursultan Nazarbayev, belong to the Great Horde.

Most Russians in Kazakhstan live in the north, where they are close to Russia. Moving the capital from Almaty in the south to Astana in the north-central region was partly designed to make the area more Kazakh-dominated. But the urban areas are still populated by more Slavs than Kazakhs. About 60 percent of Kazakhs live in the countryside. Kazakh cities grew more as a result of migration into the country than as a result of the movement of Kazakhs from the countryside to the cities.

Children of the nomadic families on the Altai Mountains.

Russian women in Semey cleaning mushrooms that were picked from the local woods for sale on the streets.

SLAVS

Russians make up the largest minority group in Kazakhstan. Most of them live in the cities of the steppes and plains in the north. For the Russians especially, living in northern Kazakhstan means that Russia is just a day's drive away. The rest of the population is made up of the other major ethnic groups of Central Asia—Uzbeks, Tajiks, and Uighurs.

The Russians began their invasion of Central Asia in the late 16th century, establishing small forts along the way and completing their advance eastward to the Pacific Ocean by the middle of the 17th century. Russian traders and soldiers arrived on the northeast edge of the Kazakh territory in the 17th century, when Cossacks established the forts that later became the cities of Oral and Atyrau. The Russian takeover was made easier when the Kazakhs, pressured by the threat of invasions from China in the east, allied themselves with the Russian Empire.

The Russian soldiers were followed by Russian settlers. They cultivated the land and formed settlements around the forts. During the 19th century, there was a flood of immigrants to the region. About 400,000 Russians arrived, followed by about a million others, including Slavs, Germans, and Jews, who arrived during the first part of the 20th century.

Another large influx of Russians and Slavs occurred between 1954 and 1956 during the Virgin and Idle Lands project that was initiated by Nikita Khrushchev. These people settled in the rich agricultural areas in the north.

Although Kazakhstan is the fourth most heavily populated of the former Soviet republics, its overall population density is low. Based on 2005 United Nations world population figures, there are about 15 people per square mile.

The distribution of the population throughout the country is not even. Most people live in the cities. The urban areas are populated by more Slavs than Kazakhs. About 43 percent of Kazakhs live in the rural areas. About half of the inhabitants of Almaty, which until 1997 was the capital city, are Kazakhs. The cities have been created more as a result of the immigration rather than because of the movement of Kazakhs from the country into the cities.

"PROBLEM" PEOPLE

Between 1935 and 1940 Russia deported about 120,000 Poles from other areas of the Soviet Union to Kazakhstan. During World War II the Soviet leader Stalin used Kazakhstan as a dumping ground for many groups of people that the Soviets regarded as "problems." The Germans who lived in the Volga region of the Soviet Union were deported because it was feared that they might help the enemy, Nazi Germany, although Germans had actually lived in the Volga region for almost two centuries. Nevertheless their loyalty to the Soviet Union was in question. They were sent to Kazakhstan and Siberia with little food to sustain them.

The Crimean Tatars were another group of people deported during the war. The Tatars were people who were descended from the Mongols and had settled in the Crimean region. Stalin was afraid that they too might help the invading German army because they had suffered under the Soviet policy of collectivization. But Nazi Germany invaded the region before the Tartars could be deported. When the Soviet Union won the war and recaptured the Crimea, the Tatars were deported to Uzbekistan and Kazakhstan as punishment. Their villages in the Crimea were destroyed and all evidence of their culture was erased. The Tatars claim that as many as 110,000 of their people died by 1946.

It is helpful to see the Kazakhs in the larger context of Central Asia. They are ethnically and linguistically linked with the other major groups in the region. The Kazakhs are the second-largest ethnic group after the Uzbeks. The other three large ethnic groups are the Tajiks, Turkmens, and the Kyrgyz. Each of these groups has given its name to one of the five republics that make up the Central Asian portion of the Commonwealth of Independent States. They share a common religion, Islam, which was brought to the southern parts of Central Asia in the seventh century and later spread north. Kazakhs, Uzbeks, Tajiks, Turkmens, and Kyrgyz are mainly Muslims. Except for the Persian Tajiks, Kazakhs and the others belong to the larger Turkic ethnic group. Again, except for the Tajiks, the others speak some form of the Turkic language. The Tajiks speak an Indo-European language.

After independence many non-Kazakhs have left Kazakhstan, going to other former Soviet republics. Many of them were technicians and skilled workers. At the same time the government encouraged Kazakhs from China and other parts of the former Soviet Union to return to their country. As a result of an uncertain future in Mongolia, Kazakhs there also returned. They were welcomed by the government and were provided with housing, plots of land, and tax exemptions for two years. There was an increase in population during the early years after independence, but this seems to have peaked, and the country is now experiencing a mild drop in population numbers.

ETHNIC TENSIONS

Independence has increased tension between the country's two largest ethnic groups: the Kazakhs and the Slavs. Slavs feel they are now at a disadvantage compared to the Kazakhs in terms of job opportunities

THE KAZAKH DIASPORA

As a result of the many migrations of Kazakhs out of their country during their troubled history, there are large concentrations of Kazakhs in many countries. In all there are more than 11 million Kazakhs. About 8 million live in Kazakhstan. The next biggest population of Kazakhs may be found in the northern Xinjiang region of China, where according to a 1990 Chinese census, there were 1.2 million of them. Other major concentrations of Kazakhs outside the country can be found in Uzbekistan, Russia, Mongolia, Tajikistan, and Ukraine. Refugees during the Soviet era fled to Afghanistan but have since left that country to settle in Turkey and Iran. In the 1950s about 5,000 Kazakhs of Chinese origin emigrated to Turkey. A very small number of Kazakhs can be found in the United States, United Kingdom, Germany, France, Sweden, and Denmark. On the Internet the U.S. Kazakh Association can be found at www.uskba.net/

and promotions. Although there are Slavic ministers in the government, many Slavs feel they will do better if they emigrate to the other CIS countries, especially Russia. The Slavs see Kazakhstan as a multiethnic home; therefore they want to enjoy equal status with the Kazakhs. On the other hand Kazakhs see their independence as a rightful claim of their homeland, which the Russians invaded and dominated for a long time.

Opposite: A Chechen refugee boy plays with his infant sister as other refugees gather in a room of a private house in Almaty.

Portrait of a family in Kazakhstan.

LIFESTYLE

Passengers boarding and leaving their trains at a railway station in Kazakhstan.

CHAPTER 7

THE IMPORTANCE OF THE FAMILY, respect for elders, and the responsibilities of belonging to a network of kinfolk and the clan are enduring values passed down through many generations of nomads, giving a Kazakh his or her identity. Although many modern Kazakhs, especially those who live in the cities, have never led a nomadic lifestyle, they are proud of this tradition.

Life in modern Kazakhstan is firmly rooted in nomadic traditions even as the country is finding a foothold in the 21st century. This is evidenced by the tall and modern skyscrapers that define the skyline of the capital city, Astana.

Children playing at the local playground in Astana. The lifestyles of the city folks are very different from those of the nomadic tribes.

THE NOMADIC LIFESTYLE

A nomad's life is essentially a difficult one. Each tribe has a hereditary route of migration and campsites that they use every year when they move their herds from winter to summer grazing. No group is allowed to use the grazing lands of another.

Nomads live at their main campsite during the winter. They normally spend four to five months a year there. The site is carefully chosen—it has to be sheltered and have ample water and grazing opportunities. Once they arrive at the campsite, they build their *yurts*, which are tent-like structures, or in some cases, they create shelters from mounds of dirt, sticks, and stones.

Winter is a period of rest. Being in one area for a few months allows the nomads to make clothes and other items that they will need during the long trek back to their summer camp.

Once the snow melts and the new grass begins to grow, the nomads begin the spring migration to their summer campsites. Travel is slow, as they stop every few days and set up camp wherever there is a source of water. They proceed in this fashion until they reach their summer camp, usually by May or June.

On reaching the summer pastures, the group divides into smaller units and spreads out so that their animals have a greater area for grazing. When they break up into smaller units, "runners" carry messages between the groups. During the summer, the campsite might be moved several times within the general area if the grass or water becomes exhausted. The nomads remain at this campsite until August or September when all groups reassemble for the long trek back to their winter site.

The distances that the nomads cover during their migration varies from region to region: anything from 124 to 186 miles (200 to 300 km) in the south to as much as 621 miles (1,000 km) in the western and central parts of the country.

Each Kazakh household has its own herd, but the animals graze together with the herds of other households. Kazakhs own both sheep and goats, which they value very much, because sheep and goats provide them with food and clothing. They are also easy to feed as they eat all kinds of grass.

But the animal that the Kazakhs truly treasure is the horse. It is the horse that makes their nomadic lifestyle possible. They can ride their horses and use them to carry household possessions. The central and southern Kazakhs often use camels instead of horses. Cattle were more commonly used in the north.

The nomads' biggest problem is the weather. If the winter is harsh, their animals will starve, especially if storms cover the grass with ice that is impenetrable. Kazakhs call this phenomenon a *zhut* (JART). Zhuts occur about once every 10 to 12 years. In the summer drought is a problem. The nomads dig shallow wells along their migration routes, and these can dry up in years when there is little rain. The salinity of the lakes and rivers on the steppes are an additional problem. As a result of this harsh and demanding life, family relationships become very important as people have to depend on each other for survival.

In modern Kazakhstan the true nomadic life is fast disappearing, but some Kazakhs do engage in a semi-nomadic life, moving their herds and flocks to summer pastures every year.

A Kazakh nomad riding his donkey cart, with the family yurt in the background.

The traditional Kazakh dwelling is the yurt. This is a dome-shaped, tent-like structure made of a flexible framework of willow wood that is covered with layers of felt for warmth. An opening at the top that can be opened and shut allows smoke from the central stove to escape and allows occupants of the yurt to control the temperature. A yurt weighs about 550 pounds (250 kg) in all. It takes about an hour and a half to put it up.

The floor is the first part to be assembled, then the walls, which are made up of several sections of wooden latticework. The lattice is made of thin, wooden strips that are crisscrossed and can be opened and shut like a concertina. These sections are tied together to make a circle. There may be as many as 12 sections needed to make up the wall of a large yurt. After these are fitted together with the door, the next step is to put up wooden posts in the middle, which will hold the roof up.

A small wooden wheel for the center of the roof is balanced on top of the posts. Then wooden spokes are radiated from the wheel to the wall. Everything is carefully tied together. Over this skeleton structure is attached a layer of canvas and blankets of felt. In the winter, thicker layers of felt are used. Another layer of canvas is thrown over the felt to keep out the rain. There is a small opening left at the very center so that air can circulate in the yurt and smoke from the cooking can escape.

Although the yurt is really one big open space, there are areas that are designated for special functions. The sleeping quarters are toward the back of the yurt while cooking is done on the stove in the center. Visitors are entertained near the front. The right side is usually reserved for the men and the left for the women.

WAY OF THE ELDERS

Age is a positive attribute and one that is associated with wisdom. Kazakhs show great respect for their elders. This is one of the binding elements of Kazakh society and is known as the way of the elders. Elders are treated with honor and deference whenever they are present, whether at home or elsewhere. Elders are always consulted to give advice, to solve problems, and to make decisions that everyone respects and obeys. In the past it was imperative to obey an elder, and anyone who did not do so was punished. In this way the social structure is maintained. The same kind of deferential attitude shown to an elder is also shown to someone seen to be in a higher social position, such as a doctor or a teacher. A student would never criticize a teacher, nor would a junior worker criticize a supervisor.

A wedding ceremony in the Zenkov Cathedral in Almaty.

MARRIAGE TIES

In the past girls married at 13 or 14 and men when they were one or two years older. Today, however, the bride and groom have to be 18 years of age and both have to agree to the marriage. Traditionally the engagement ceremony involves the groom's parents visiting the bride's parents to discuss a payment for the bride and her dowry. The dowry includes new clothes for the bride, a carpet, bed linen, and other household items, and a big trunk to hold these items. The payment depends on the wealth of the groom's family and is often paid in livestock. It can range from a few hundred sheep, camels, horses, and cows to several thousand cattle. If the bride's family agrees to the amount, the groom's father gives her father earrings and owl's feathers. Five or six relatives of the groom then visit the bride's father for a meal. The father gives each of them an animal as a sign of goodwill. The groom and his parents also give the bride's parents and relatives presents on the wedding day. Sometimes, thousands of guests are invited to the wedding.

RIGHTS OF INHERITANCE

Each of the three hordes is subdivided into patrilineal lines—that is, inheritance, descent, and kinship follows the male line. When a man dies, he passes on the family responsibility to his eldest son, and his herds are divided among all his sons.

Historically women did not have a share of the inheritance. The exceptions were an unmarried daughter, who received part of the livestock; and a widow, who took charge of the livestock if her sons were still too young. Although women did not have inheritance rights, they were strong members of the society and were consulted on all matters of importance.

In modern Kazakhstan women have gained equality with men and their family and inheritance rights are fully protected by law.

NETWORKING

As a result of the ties of marriage and kinship, a Kazakh man can always count on having the support of his relatives. He knows he can draw on the resources and the network of his relatives in times of need. He has three

Young professionals working together in the city.

WOMEN IN KAZAKHSTAN

Kazakhs are proud of their women. Traditionally the woman's ultimate goal in life was to marry and raise a family. When a girl was young, she was trained in the duties of keeping a home and looking after her younger brothers and sisters. She looked forward to doing the same after marriage—taking care of her husband and her home. Many wives would not allow their husbands to do what they considered the wife's chores about the home. A wife loved and respected her husband while expecting to be treated with equal respect by him. But as has happened all over the world, this traditional view has changed with a more modern outlook, one that is giving Kazakh women more than a homebound role in society. Although most Kazakh women would still insist that their families, homes, and children come first in their lives, they no longer bear these burdens alone. Many women work outside the home, are highly educated, and are career women or professionals. They expect men to share household responsibilities with them.

networks of relatives—his father's relatives, his mother's relatives, and his wife's relatives.

It is not unusual for a Kazakh living in the city to have his distant cousin suddenly arrive from the countryside for a visit. He is obliged to provide a meal and even a bed for his relative, who usually comes with gifts.

These obligations are extended to include a whole network of relationships, so a Kazakh may also call on the services and help of old friends, schoolmates, and fellow workers. The bigger and stronger a family's social connections are, the more favors can be requested. This is useful when a family member needs to get a job, obtain a permit, bypass some government regulation, obtain medical services, get a discount for a purchase, or send a child to college.

Young Kazakhs dressed in their country's traditional costumes.

HEALTH AND SOCIAL WELFARE

Kazakhstan had a well-established public health system that provided free medical care not only in the cities but also in the remote regions. This was a legacy from the Soviet system. However, the difficult years that immediately followed independence affected this public health service. The main problem was a lack of funds.

In 1993 Kazakhstan was rated below average among the former Soviet republics in terms of medical systems, pharmaceutical supply, research and development, and medical sanitation. A poor diet, environmental pollution, and inadequate health-care services are reasons for this. Life expectancy is also low compared with the West but has improved since the early days after independence, although it has not reached pre-independence levels. The average lifespan now of Kazakh men is 62 years, and 73 for women.

The 1995 constitution guarantees free, basic health care, but in practice, this has been difficult to attain. Reduced public funding, deregulations, and privatization have resulted in an inequitable health supply. Patients now find that they have to pay for many of the medical and pharmaceutical supplies they need. There is better access to health care in the cities than in the rural areas.

In 1992 government spending on health-care services was 1.6 percent of the country's GDP (gross domestic product). The lack of funds meant that

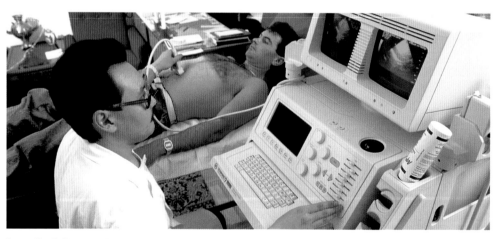

A medical diagnostic center in Karaganda.

doctors, nurses, and other medical personnel were paid very little and that sometimes these already low wages were not paid. As a result many people in the medical profession left Kazakhstan for other republics. But as with many other aspects of life in Kazakhstan, the government hopes to improve the situation. In 2005 the World Health Organization (WHO) recorded that government spending on health-care services had increased to almost 4 percent in 2005. But the challenge is to use this money to provide better quality and more efficient health care.

The population of Kazakhstan has continued to decrease in number since 1991. Fewer babies are being born (16.6 births per 1,000 population estimated in 2009) while the death rate is increasing (9.39 per 1,000 population estimated in 2009). Cardiovascular diseases, tuberculosis, and HIV/AIDS are some of the country's major health problems.

Since the 1990s the declining birthrate has become a matter of state concern, and Kazakh nationalist parties have tried to ban birth control and abortions. In 1995 Nazarbayev stated that one of the country's goals is to create a society in which a woman is encouraged to work at home and raise her children. However, this makes it difficult for women to rise to senior positions in government or private enterprises, despite the fact that the constitution of 1995 safeguards against discrimination of all kinds.

EDUCATION

Education is mandatory and free through secondary school. Before independence Russian was the only official language. After independence Kazakh also became an official language. In the early 1990s schools continued to teach in Russian because there was a shortage of Kazakh textbooks and teachers. With increasing emphasis on Kazakh, more Russians are sending their children to Russia for their education. Local teachers are required to have a fluent knowledge of Kazakh, and this has led to more Kazakh than Slav teachers in primary and secondary schools.

The USSR detonated nearly 500 nuclear bombs at the numerous test sites in northeast Kazakhstan in the 1950s. Thousands of villagers and their children still suffer the consequences of the early radioactive experiments.

Kazakhstan has a very high literacy rate of more than 99 percent. Both boys and girls tend to remain in school until they are about 15 years old. Private education is allowed but is closely supervised and controlled by the state. More than 90 percent of children of primary and secondary school age attend school. After secondary education, students have many choices for postsecondary education as there are many universities and colleges to choose from. These offer degrees in the traditional academic fields as well as engineering, economics, management, agriculture, and research. Of these, the largest is the Al-Farabi State National University in Almaty.

There was a reorganization of the school curriculum and changes in the textbooks after independence. Kazakh history, culture, and literature are getting greater attention. This has an effect not only in schools, but also in institutions of higher learning. The Kazakhstan Academy of Sciences has renewed its focus on matters that are of importance to the country, in the disciplines of the sciences and the humanities. Many research papers once considered incompatible with communist ideology have now been published either for the first time or for the first time after many years of being out of print.

Children from an elementary school in Aralsk. The literacy rate of the population is very high in Kazakhstan.

IMPORTANCE OF FEASTS

Connected with kinship bonds is the practice of holding feasts. Feasting and the giving of gifts that accompanies them take up a large proportion of a Kazakh's time and money. It is not merely because celebrations are enjoyed and that everyone loves to receive gifts that Kazakhs do often. There are very important social reasons behind this custom.

Feasts are usually held when important life events take place, such as a birth, death, marriage, or an important birthday. It would be unthinkable and almost a matter of family dishonor should a grandmother's 60th birthday, for example, not be celebrated in this manner.

Besides the pure happiness of celebrating, these feasts are a means by which Kazakhs establish and maintain their social status. A family that is putting on a celebration calls upon its relations and friends to help out, and this help is returned when their friends or other family members have to hold a celebration. Gifts are always exchanged at these events—guests come bearing gifts and are given something in return.

This tradition of feasting and gift giving puts a strain on Kazakhs in times of economic difficulty, especially now when the country is trying to find its own independent way in the world. Inflation has cut into the worth of a family's income, so that the same number of dollars buys them less. Despite this there is no question of not giving a gift if an occasion calls for it. Kazakhs know that when they invite people to celebrate they will be invited in return. And when they give a gift, they will also receive.

Another consequence of feasting and gift giving in Kazakh social life is that it is the subject of much conversation and gossip. Months before and after the event has happened, people will still remember the lavishness of a feast, how much meat there was, who the honored guests were, what gifts were exchanged. The value of the gifts is also discussed and evaluated, were they imported or foreign goods which meant they were more valued, or were they homemade or Soviet-produced. Common gift items are clothing or cloth, jewelry, rugs and carpets, household goods, and livestock.

RELIGION

The Astana Central National Mosque in Kazakhstan.

CHAPTER 8

AZAKHSTAN IS MAINLY A MUSLIM country. Forty-seven percent of the population, mostly Kazakhs, belong to this religion. Despite the importance of Islam in the society, it is not the national religion. The 1995 constitution states that Kazakhstan is a secular state and protects religious freedom. Kazakhstan is the only state in Central Asia that does not give Islam special status.

The ornate interior of the Zenkov Cathedral in Almaty.

ARABS BRING ISLAM

Islam was introduced to the area in the eighth century when the Arabs invaded the southern part of the country. However, many of the nomads did not become Muslims until the 18th century. The religion was practiced more by those who lived in the cities, mostly the traders, than by the pastoral people who had little knowledge of Islam's teachings and practices. The nomads' contact with Islam probably came from the holy men who traveled the steppes, following the Silk Road. Since they did not understand Arabic, they could not gain direct knowledge of the teachings of the Koran, the holy book of the Muslims.

This change to Islam was not a difficult one because before Islam, Kazakhs believed in one sky god they called Tengri (*Tanir* in Kazakh). Since their ancient beliefs did not conflict with the new religion, the two merged easily and Islam became their new faith. In areas where Islam conflicted with the animistic and shamanistic beliefs, the ancient practices were abandoned without much concern.

Islam had a greater influence on people's lives after they moved into settlements and sent their children to school. Children were sent to Muslim schools and were taught the precepts of Islam and its ideology.

Listening to the teachings of the Muslim imam, or religious leader.

ISLAM'S FIVE PILLARS

Islam, Christianity, and Judaism have prophets in common. The biblical patriarch Abraham had two sons, Isaac and Ishmael. Arabs believe they are descendants of Ishmael, while Jews are descendants of Isaac. Muslims believe God sent many prophets to teach the people—Abraham, Moses, David, Jesus, and Muhammad—and that Muhammad was the most important and last of the prophets. God (Allah) also sent the angel Gabriel to reveal his message to the people, and his words are written in the holy book called the Koran.

A true Muslim must follow the Five Pillars of Islam—the shahadah (sha-HAHD-ah), the declaration in Arabic that there is only one God, Allah, and that Muhammad is the messenger of Allah; prayer or salat (sa-LAHT); giving alms or zakat (zah-KART); fasting or sawm (sa-AHM); and going on pilgrimage or hajj. Giving alms, the third pillar, is intended to help the poor. Muslims give zakat once a year to the mosque or a Muslim welfare organization. Fasting is observed for the whole of Ramadan, which is the ninth month of the Islamic calendar. Muslims consider this the holy month. During this month Muslims are not allowed to eat, drink, smoke, or have sex during the day. At night they may resume these normal activities. Finally a pilgrimage is required at least once in a person's lifetime to the holy city of Mecca. This is the hajj.

In addition, at all times of the year, Muslims are not allowed to eat pork or drink alcohol, gamble, or be unkind to others. They also have to say their daily prayers. Muslims must pray five times a day—before dawn, at noon, in the mid-afternoon, after sunset, and before going to bed. When it is time to pray, a man called the muezzin calls the people to pray. His voice can be heard coming from the mosque five times a day. Muslims bow and face Mecca when they pray. On Fridays they must go to the mosque for prayers. It is mostly the men who pray at the mosque. When women go they have a separate place in which to pray. Muslim prayers are usually said in Arabic.

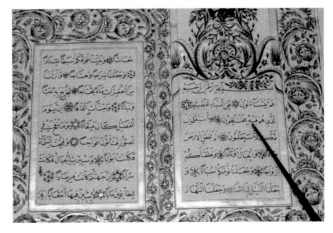

But when Kazakhstan became part of the communist Soviet Union, all forms of religion were discouraged. This policy lasted for several decades until 1991, when the Soviet Union fell apart. Under the communists and when there was active repression of religion, many Kazakhs, although they were Muslims, never visited a mosque or read the Koran. During the late 1920s and the 1930s the Soviet government became extremely anti-religion. Religious leaders were seen as influential figures, especially in the countryside, and the authorities wanted to get rid of them so that people would remain loyal only to the communist regime. The government closed down the mosques and religious schools and organizations and arrested the clergy. Nevertheless the Muslim clerics continued to operate underground, and the people continued to sympathize with their religious leaders. After independence, the religious climate improved significantly. Kazakhs generally are now free to practice any religion.

The New Mangali Mosque in Atyrau.

ISLAM IN KAZAKHSTAN TODAY

Although government statistics state that as many as 47 percent of the population claim to be Muslims, a large number of these people actually do not follow the precepts of their professed religion. This could be because they once followed a nomadic lifestyle, with little need for a central religious force. Truly staunch and practicing Muslims make up a very small percentage of the population. Most Kazakhs are just nominally Muslim and do not go to pray at the mosque. They may celebrate the Muslim festivals, but these celebrations have greater social than religious significance. Only those Kazakhs who are devout and able to afford it go on pilgrimages to Muslim holy places in Central Asia or Saudi Arabia.

ORTHODOX CHRISTIANS AND OTHERS

The other dominant religion in the country is the Russian Orthodox Church. Most of the Orthodox Christians are Russians, Ukrainians, and other Slavs. They make up about 44 percent of the population. The main church in Almaty is Saint Nicholas Cathedral. There are also Protestants, mainly Baptists, as well as some Roman Catholics, Jews, and others.

With its majestic gold domes, this Russian Orthodox church in the old town of Atyrau dates back to 1888.

The Eastern Orthodox Church is one of the three main branches of Christianity. The other two are the Roman Catholic Church and the Protestant Church. Today the Orthodox Church is made up of many local and national churches, each of which has a head called a patriarch. The major churches are in Greece, Russia, Eastern Europe, and western Asia.

The Church believes that it is faithful to the teachings of the Apostles of Christ and that it is free from errors in doctrinal matters. Orthodox churches are beautifully decorated with many religious images called icons. Easter is the most important time of the year, and every Sunday is considered a celebration of Christ's resurrection from the dead.

Orthodox Christians go to church every Sunday and on feast days. The church services are sung or chanted, and people usually stand during the services. There are several times during the year that fasts are observed. During these periods, the believer is not allowed to eat meat or dairy products, and sometimes not even fish. Devout people also fast every Wednesday and Friday.

ANCIENT PRACTICES

Most Kazakhs did not adopt Islam as a religion until the 18th century, and it was not strongly enforced or practiced by those who continued to live a nomadic life. Many nomads continue to observe pre-Islamic religious practices, such as shamanism, animism, and ancestor worship. These three practices are interrelated. Since the Kazakhs are pastoral and nomadic, it is easy to understand why they hold these beliefs. Their lifestyle and well-being depend on the weather and having healthy animals. Kazakhs believe that various animals, the Earth, and celestial bodies such as the sun and the moon are inhabited by the spirits of the dead. They also believe that there is a struggle for power between the forces of good and evil. When they embraced Islam, the Prophet Muhammad and his teachings became the embodiment of the force of good.

Unlike Muslims in Middle Eastern countries, Kazakh Muslims are more informal about their Islamic beliefs.

In animism different spirits are believed to inhabit animals. For the Kazakhs these are the animals they are close to—sheep, cows, horses, and camels. Spirits are also present in the elements of fire, water, and earth, and may be contacted and asked for help. The nomads offer prayers to the water spirit in times of drought, to the earth spirit to ensure good weather, and to the animal spirits when the health of their livestock is threatened.

The shaman or medicine man is a wise person with special powers. He is able to mediate between the spirits and the people. Many Kazakhs are superstitious and will wear charms of holy objects to ward off evil spirits. They believe that it is possible to cast an evil eye on somebody you hate in order to hurt him. Trips to the graves of holy people and ancestors are made to ask for advice or to receive a blessing.

Because the traditional lifestyle is based on the rearing of animals, many customs and beliefs relate to livestock. When someone wishes another person ill, he will curse the other person's livestock with poor health. For instance a Kazakh might curse an enemy in this manner: "May you never own your livestock and be unable to migrate with your people" or "May you have neither horse nor camel, but always have to travel on foot." In the same way blessings are expressed as an abundance of animals or a wish for their successful fertility. A Kazakh wishing someone well might offer this blessing: "May God bless you with one thousand sheep and lambs." When Kazakhs greet one another, it is considered polite to inquire after the health of the other person's animals—for example, "Are you and your livestock healthy?"

RELIGIOUS CLIMATE TODAY

Since independence there has been an increase in religious activity. All religious groups have gained a new freedom to practice. Many more people now claim to be religious, and there is an increase in the number of religious organizations in the country.

Some groups that were illegal during Soviet times, such as Jehovah's Witnesses and several fundamentalist Christian groups, have been allowed into the country.

Snow camels are sometimes kept on farms. Kazakhs believe spirits live in the bodies of the animals with which they are constantly in contact.

Islam is becoming increasingly important in modern Kazakh society. A number of mosques and religious schools have been constructed with financial aid from the Muslim countries of Saudi Arabia, Turkey, and Egypt. But although the Nazarbayev government is aware of the potential foreign investment it may receive from the Muslim countries of the Middle East, it has been careful to maintain a balance between the Muslim East and the Christian West. When President Nazarbayev made a trip to the Muslim holy city of Mecca in 1994, he also visited the Roman Catholic primate, Pope John Paul II, in the Vatican.

From 1985 to 1990 the number of mosques more than doubled, from 25 to 60. An Islamic institute has been opened in Almaty. Since 1990 there has been an explosion of mosque building: There are now some 4,000 mosques believed to be functioning in the country. Loudspeakers on mosques broadcast the call to prayer five times a day and thus can be heard more and more in Kazakh cities.

Even President Nazarbayev makes occasional references to Allah in his speeches. Nevertheless the state remains secular, that is, there is no official state religion. This is probably helpful in a country such as Kazakhstan where there are so many ethnic communities other than Kazakhs. The other communities might feel imposed on and would be extremely sensitive to any signs of a government favoring a dominant culture and religion.

LANGUAGE

Elderly men enjoying each other's company
as they reminisce about the past.

KAZAKH AND RUSSIAN ARE THE two officially recognized languages in Kazakhstan. Kazakh is the state language of the country, but the 1995 constitution recognized Russian as the language used in conducting government and business affairs.

Kazakhstan is different from the other Central Asian republics of the CIS in that the majority of its people speak Russian. Only about 40 percent of all Kazakhs speak their own language. About a third of the other Turkic-speaking people—the Uzbeks, Tatars, and Uighurs—also speak Kazakh, while fewer than 10 percent of the rest of the population—Russians, Ukrainians, Belorussians, Koreans, and Germans—have bothered to master Kazakh.

Russian is commonly used in business and communication. It is also the language of instruction in higher institutions, and parents prefer to send their children to schools that teach in Russian, to prepare them for higher education.

When Kazakhstan became independent, the language problem became a contentious one. President Nazarbayev tried to make Kazakh the only official language in the hopes of ensuring its survival as a language. But Russians in the country were afraid that it would lead to discrimination against them if Kazakh should become the only legal state language. There was also the danger that a strong Kazakh language policy would cause skilled Russians, Slavs, and Germans to leave the country. However, the government has relaxed a little in its language policy, giving Kazakh a special status as the state language while

ESTABLISHING AN OFFICIAL LANGUAGE

The process of establishing Kazakh as the preeminent language in the country has necessitated a major redesign and revamping of the educational curriculum and the development of textbooks in Kazakh. The study of Kazakh history, literature, and culture, which used to be ignored and even suppressed during the Soviet era, is now receiving the attention that is due to it. The Kazakhstan Academy of Sciences now considers its major focus to be research into Kazakh sciences and humanities. Where once scholars had to be careful in their choice of research subjects and how they interpreted their findings, as these had to be in accordance to the demands of Soviet censors, these restrictions have now been lifted. Many studies that were previously suppressed have recently come back into print.

making Russian an official language. There are both Kazakh and Russian medium schools in which the other language is taught as a second language. Russian is still the main language for communication and is likely to remain so in the near future. It is the language that helps the many different ethnic groups in the country communicate with one another.

KAZAKH

Kazakh became a written language in the 1860s. At that time Arabic script was used for it. In 1929 the Latin, or Roman, script was introduced, and in 1940 Cyrillic script was used. Initiated by Joseph Stalin this alphabet unified

Біз - бабалары басының қадірін арттыруды басты мұрат санаған елдің баласымыз!

Billboard advertisement showing important historical people of Kazakhstan on a main street in Satpaev in Atyrau.

The word Kazakh was found in a Turkish-Arabic dictionary in 1245. It means "independent, free, wanderer, exile," and according to one of the interpretations, it refers to a free person who broke away from his people to lead the life of an adventurer or a group of nomads. The nomads in Kazakhstan were originally called Uzbek-Kazakhs because they were members of the Uzbek tribe who had broken away from the group. They began to drop the word Uzbek after 1468 when groups of Uzbek-Kazakhs united in victory against the Uzbek tribe. Burunduk Khan (1473—1511) was called the ruler of the "Kazakhs."

the written language of the Soviet Central Asian republics with that of Russia. Modified in 1954 the 42-letter script now uses 33 letters of the standard Russian alphabet and some symbols specific to the Kazakh language. With independence Kazakhstan has toyed with the idea of reintroducing the Latin-based alphabet.

Kazakh is a Turkic language with strong influences from other historical languages in the region, such as Arabic, Perisan, Tatar, and Mongolian. It is part of the Nogai-Kipchak subgroup of northeastern Turkic languages.

Kazakh has several dialects. The main ones are Northeastern Kazakh, Southern Kazakh, and Western Kazakh. These dialects are quite similar to each other.

A respectful way to address an elder in Kazakh is to attach the suffix *-ke* to the shortened form of the person's name—for example, Nursultan would be shortened to *Nureke.*

Kazakh men of various origins looking through a book.

KAZAKH OR RUSSIAN

The government conducted a study in 1996 to assess the state of the language among the people. The study examined how the various ethnic groups viewed and used both Kazakh and Russian.

First of all, it found that the majority of people, no matter what ethnic group they belonged to, were effectively bilingual, that is, they could speak their own language and spoke, read, and wrote Russian as their second language. The exceptions were the Russians and the Slavs, who tended to speak only Russian.

Kazakhstan is different from the other four Central Asian republics of the CIS in that the majority of its people speak Russian. Not as many people were fluent in the Kazakh language. Although almost all Kazakhs were able to speak their language with varying degrees of success, and about a third of the other Turkic-speaking people—that is, the Uzbeks, Tatars, and Uighurs—also spoke the language, only a very small percentage, less than 10 percent of the other people—Russians, Ukrainians, Belarusians, Koreans, and Germans—had bothered to master Kazakh. The study also found that Kazakh was spoken more often in the rural districts than in the cities. The younger generation of all ethnic groups, however, had a greater knowledge of Kazakh than their elders.

However, it was agreed by more than half the people surveyed that it was important for their children to learn Kazakh as well as Russian. But despite the belief that it was desirable to learn Kazakh, there are practical problems that limit the realization of this goal. Perhaps the biggest problem is that the language of instruction in institutions of higher learning is Russian. Russian is also a world language and the language for science and technology. Parents, when choosing what language they want their children to be instructed in, invariably give this greater consideration. They prefer to send their children to schools that will prepare them for a higher secondary education in Russian.

THE MEDIA

The main newspapers in Kazakhstan are the national *Egemen Kazakhstan*, published in Kazakh; the Russian-language *Kazakstanskaya Pravda*, the organ of the council of ministers; and *Sovety Kazakstana*, the organ of parliament.

There are many other newspapers, and although these enjoy a certain amount of freedom and expression, guaranteed in the 1995 constitution, the government is increasing control over what is being published, while not engaging in outright censorship.

A newspaper stand in Almaty.

Some private newspapers have been refused publishing facilities at the government presses for various "technical" reasons, and sponsors of erring newspapers have faced investigations or had financial pressure brought on them. The law explicitly forbids any personal criticism of the president or his family.

Several newspapers have political links. *The Respublika* was published by the Socialist Party until it was sold to a commercial enterprise. The *NKK* is the paper of the People's Congress Party.

The largest independent newspaper, *The Panorama*, is owned by some of the largest businesses in the country. The newspaper tries to focus an objective eye on political and economic issues. Two other purely commercial newspapers are the tabloid *Karavan* and the *Almaty Business News*. Both are published by a Russian-owned company, called Karavan.

Radio and television are extremely important in linking the distant parts of the country together. Besides the national broadcasting service, foreign broadcasting stations in the neighboring countries of Uzbekistan and Kyrgyzstan together with Moscow stations give Kazakh listeners more choices in television programs.

ARTS

A mural in Almaty shows old Kazakh men playing traditional instruments such as the two-stringed *dombra* and the three-stringed *kobiz*.

K AZAKH CULTURE IS RICHLY endowed with fine arts such as painting and sculpture, as well as music, theater, and literature. In addition it has a well-established and important tradition of oral history through which modern Kazakhs have been able to maintain their link with the past.

Kazakhstan ensures that it recognizes the contribution of its artists by awarding them various titles such as Merited Artist, People's Artist, and Honored Artist of Kazakhstan, Badges of Honor, and Certificates of Honor.

Dancers in their traditional Kazakh costumes.

ORAL TRADITIONS

The statue of a famous *akyn*, Jambyl. This statue, situated in Almaty, was sculpted by a well-known Kazakh artist named Khakimzhan Naurzbayev.

Before the mid-19th century most Kazakh customs and traditions were part of an oral tradition of stories and poetry. Storytellers and singers, called *akyns* (A-keens), and lyric poets, known as *jyrau* (JAI-rau), were entrusted with the responsibility of memorizing the stories, legends, and history of the Kazakh people and keeping their cultural history alive by reciting it and passing it on to the next generation of storytellers.

Akyns are storytellers who traveled from one nomadic camp to another reciting the epic stories of Kazakh history and legend. Many of the stories tell of the exploits of legendary warriors and their struggle against Mongol Kalmyks. The stories are often recited with the accompaniment of traditional instruments such as the drum. The Kalmyks were pastoral nomads and descendents of the Mongols who lived in the eastern and southeastern parts of the country. They fought the Kazakhs for control of the land in the 17th century.

But not all stories tell of battles or warrior heroes. Some are romantic tales, such as the love story of Enlik and Kebek, who chose death in the face of family opposition to their love, while others, such as the most famous love story, *Kyz-Zhibek*, are lyrical love poems.

The poems and poetic songs of the khanate period survived because they were preserved orally until the late 19th century, when they were recorded by Kazakh intellectuals. But the Soviets suppressed these records until the 1960s.

KYZ-ZHIBEK

A popular Kazakh story is that of a young woman, Kyz-Zhibek, who had been promised to a suitor. But she and Tulegen, the young chief of the Lesser Horde meet and fall in love. The rejected suitor then kills Tulegen. In revenge Kyz-Zhibek's brother kills the suitor. The story then takes a break until eight years later when Sansizbai, Tulegen's younger brother, returns from the war and learns of his brother's death. Kyz-Zhibek was then about to be married to a Kalmyk prince. Sansizbai kills the prince and escapes with Kyz-Zhibek. He marries her and thus fulfils his duty and honors the memory of his slain brother.

The *jyrau* are very respected members of their tribes and honored as elders. They are often part of the ruler's retinue of followers. Unlike the *akyns*, the *jyrau* have contact with the world at large, and their poetry contains Islamic elements with references to Allah.

One famous poet is Asan Kangi, who lived from 1370 to 1465. He served the Mongolian court of the Golden Horde. Other notable poets also include Dosbambet Jhyrau (1490—1523) and Jhalkiz Jhyrau (1465—1560).

Teenage girls performing with the *dombra*.

MUSICAL TRADITION

Music plays an equally big role in Kazakh life, complementing the oral tradition of storytelling. It is a means of entertainment, and no festival is complete without a band of musicians playing. But, together with storytelling, music is also a way of recording tribal history in song, and it has magical qualities when it is employed by the shaman or medicine man.

A folk orchestra performing at an event in Kazakhstan.

Unique to the Kazakhs is the musical-oral tradition of *Ajtys*. This is a competition requiring the contestants, both men and women, to improvise with poetry and music. Two contestants try to outdo each other in composing the better song.

The nomads used songs and instrumental music called *kujs* to pass on their traditions from one generation to the next. For example each seasonal migration was blessed by a special song sung by an elder, called the *aksakal*.

There are more than 50 Kazakh musical instruments—string, wind, and percussion. They are made from wood, metal, reed, leather, horn, and horsehair. The most common string instruments that Kazakhs play are the two-stringed, lute-like instrument called a *dombra* and the *kobyz*, another lute-like instrument with three strings. Some older lutes have strings that are made of horsehair and others of silk. The *kobyz* is like a violin; its body is made of one piece of wood and the strings are played with a bow. Another string instrument is the *zhetigen*, which has a rectangular wooden body and seven strings made of horsehair. It is used mainly as a solo instrument or as an accompanying instrument in folk orchestras and ensembles.

The *sybyzgy* is a wind instrument. Commonly used by traditional musicians, it is made of reed or wood and resembles two small wooden flutes put together. The *adyrna* is also a wind instrument. Although it is basically a musical instrument, hunters often use it because the whistle-like sound that is made by the *adyrna* resembles the cries of birds and other animals.

There are several percussion instruments. The *dangyra* is similar to the tambourine. One side is covered with leather, and the inner rim of the instrument is lined with metal pendants that produce clacking sounds when the instrument is struck. Two drum-like instruments are the *dauylpaz* and the *dabyl*. Both are beaten with the hand or a whip and are often used for signaling in the army and for hunting.

Many Kazakh children start learning music at a very young age.

The *asatayak* is used in shamanistic rituals. It is a wooden staff or rod about 3 feet (1 m) long with metal pendants at the top. When shaken, it produces a rattling sound.

Traditional Kazakh folk singers often accompany their performances on the *dombra* or *kobyz*. There are many traditional folk songs that are sung on special occasions, such as the *koshtasu*, a song of farewell for close friends and family; the *yestirtu*, sung to announce the death of someone dear; the *zhoktau*, a song of lamentation; and the *konil aitu*, a song to comfort those who are grieving.

The Museum of Kazakh Musical Instruments in Almaty houses a unique collection of traditional Kazakh musical instruments. The museum also displays the personal musical instruments of Abay Kunanbayev and other famous Kazakh musicians. The wooden museum building itself is of artistic and historical interest. It is the achievement of the architect Andrei Zenkov, who built Zenkov Cathedral, another totally wooden building. The museum was built in 1907.

The lush interior of a traditional Kazakh yurt. Carpets are a common sight in Kazakhstan, and people like to decorate their homes with colorful felt carpets.

TEXTILES

Kazakh arts and crafts have a long tradition. The people are well known for their beautiful embroidery work on all types of daily and ceremonial articles, such as the velvet vest that is part of the Kazakh traditional dress.

Multicolored threads are combined with beads and stones to decorate items made of cloth, leather, felt, and other materials.

Carpet making is another tradition for which Kazakhs are famous. The northeastern part of the country is well known for this craft. Many Kazakh houses are decorated with handmade felt carpets and rugs of intricate colors and geometric designs.

The process of making a felt carpet is elaborate. It begins with the cleaning and dying of the wool. The dyed wool is then laid on a mat of hay and reeds (called *shij*) harvested from the steppes, wet down, and then walked on by everyone in the household. This trampling mats and fuses the wool fibers. The designs are then cut out of different colored felts and combined. This arrangement is then covered by the reed mat and stepped on again until the sections stick to each other. When the carpet is uncovered, the youngest daughter in the family sews everything together.

SILVERSMITHING

Silversmithing as a Kazakh craft reached its height in the late 19th and early 20th centuries. The silversmiths were kept busy by the wealthy, who required jewelry to complement their ornate costumes. The designs of Kazakh jewelry are similar to those of other Central Asian societies, such as the Turkmen and Tatars. Plant and animal motifs are used widely, as are geometric patterns, including circles, triangles, and dots. The silversmiths are skilled in engraving. Intricate filigree is one of the hallmarks of fine Kazakh jewelry in which delicate lacy designs are created with gold and silver wire. Further ornamentation is achieved by making use of precious and semiprecious stones for color and detail. Saddles and stirrups are lovingly created and decorated with silverwork.

NATURE PAINTERS

Creativity remains a part of the Kazakh tradition to this day. The Union of Kazakhstani Artists is the country's largest artistic organization, gathering together more than 600 painters, sculptors, folk artists, craftspeople, and other creative people.

Popular subjects for artists are scenes from nature: landscapes, especially the steppes; the changing seasons; people in the city and in nomadic settings; and portraits of famous Kazakhs, such as Abay Kunanbayev.

Artists who have achieved distinction are awarded the title of "People's Artist of Kazakhstan." Of these Abylkhan Kasteyev (1904—73) is well known, being a pioneer of Kazakh painting. He painted idealized images of collectivization and the Virgin Lands program. Among his major works are the paintings *A Hunter with a Golden Eagle*, *An Alpine Skating Rink*, and *Summer Pasture of Chalkude*. Two other "People's Artists" are sculptor Khakimzhan Naurzbayev (b. 1925) and painter, cinema, and theater artist Gulfairus Ismailova (b. 1929). Several of Naurzbayev's sculptures—monuments to Abay, Jambyl, and other famous Kazakhs—can be found in the city of Almaty. Ismailova's works include the film setting for the Kazakh epic love story of Kyz-Zhibek. She has also created stage sets for the operas *Aida* by Verdi, *Iolanta* by P. Chaikovsky, and *Regal Bride* by Rimsky-Korsakov.

Many Kazakh cultural figures were also politically active during the Soviet era. Novelist Anuar Alimzhanov was president of the last Soviet Congress of People's Deputies; poets Mukhtar Shakhanov and Olzhas Suleymenov were co-presidents of the political party the Popular Congress of Kazakhstan. Suleymenov was the leader of the Respublika opposition coalition in the parliament of 1994-95.

The state Museum of National Musical Instruments was founded in 1980 in Almaty.

MUSEUMS AND THEATERS

Almaty is a lively center of Kazakh art and culture, with many theaters and museums. The Abay Academic Opera and Ballet House, which was established in 1934, stages Kazakh operas and ballets, as well as Western productions such as *Swan Lake*. There are also theaters that showcase the artistic traditions of other communities in the country, such as the Lermontov State Academic Russian Theater, and Korean State Musical Comedy Theater. The Korean Theater, originally formed in Vladivostok in 1932, arrived in Kzyl-Orda in 1937, when Koreans were deported by the Russians to Kazakhstan; the theater was moved to Almaty in 1968.

Kazakhs love museums. The Central Museum in Almaty houses a permanent collection of archaeological finds from all over the country, historical artifacts relating to ancient, modern, and natural history, and the history of the major ethnic communities in the country. There is an art museum with crafts, art, and paintings, an Archaeology Museum, Geology Museum, Nature Museum, and even a Museum of Books.

The A. Kasteyev Museum of Fine Arts was established with a beginning collection of almost 200 art works by Russian and European artists in 1935. Today it also has a section of traditional Kazakh crafts, jewelry, and clothing, as well as Chinese, European, and Kazakh paintings.

WRITERS

Abay Kunanbayev (1845—1904) is probably the best-known literary figure in Kazakh history. He was born in the Chingiz-Tau Mountains, south of the town of Semey in northeastern Kazakhstan. Although Kunanbayev never left his native land, he was very well educated and knowledgeable about the world. He spoke several languages, among them Russian, Arabic, and Persian. Kunanbayev spent three years in an Islamic school, then taught, translated Russian literature into Kazakh, and wrote poetry. He was a nationalist who promoted Kazakh cultural identity. He spoke out strongly for the need to educate the young in order to create a moral and spiritual world. Kunanbayev idealized the traditional Kazakh life, while also advocating progress through collaborating with the Russians. Through his work, Kazakh earned its place as a literary language.

The great Kazakh poet Abay Kunanbayev.

Mukhtar Auezov (1897—1961) was the son of a nomadic family. He was a writer, literary critic, historian, and linguist. Through his writings he gave immortality to the life and culture of his people and country. He learned the power of the written word early in life. As a child he was amazed to discover that Kazakh stories and songs could be written and preserved on paper. His greatest book is the epic called *The Path of Abay* or *Abay's Way*. In it he explores the life and philosophy of the poet Abay Kunanbayev, paying homage to the poet he revered above all others. Auezov died at the age of 64 in Moscow.

Furniture is often decorated with fretwork made of wood, stone, or bone.

LEISURE

People skating at Medeo skating rink, which is in the middle of the mountains in Kazakhstan.

CHAPTER 11

THE HORSE IS CENTRAL TO THE Kazakh traditional lifestyle, so it is not surprising that many leisure activities and sports have to do with the display of good horsemanship. Kazakhs are exceptional horsemen. Children learn to ride almost as soon as they can walk. Jumping onto a horse and riding out on the steppes is as commonplace as riding a bicycle around the block in America.

Many traditional Kazakh games are based on the nomadic lifestyle and are meant to teach the people life skills, how to be resourceful, resilient, healthy, strong, and smart.

A runner jogs past a sports complex in Astana.

COURTSHIP GAME

There are a number of traditional games that Kazakhs play on horseback. One is a catch-me-if-you-can game of tag that boys and girls sometimes play. It is called *kyz kuu* (KISS-ku) or "overtake the girl." When a boy catches a girl, he wins a kiss from her. If he doesn't catch her, then she gets to hit him with her riding whip.

KAZAKH POLO

Kokpar is a very popular game in Kazakhstan. It is a wild, free-for-all scramble by Kazakhs on horseback who fight for possession of the carcass of a goat. Perhaps the game that is most similar to *kokpar* is polo. The chase on horseback is the same, but there the similarity ends. Instead of a polo ball, the headless carcass of a goat is tossed around. As many as a thousand participants can take part in the chase. There are no boundaries; the action can extend out over the steppes. The game supposedly originated as a sacrificial tradition where a goat was killed in order to obtain the blessings of the spirits. After the game, there would be a grand feast and musical performances.

Men playing *kokpar*, the national sport of Kazakhstan. Two teams compete on horseback to carry and drop a goat carcass over a line on the playing field.

SILVER COIN TEST

Another time-honored game that tests one's horsemanship is *kumis alu*, which means "pick up the coin." The aim is for the rider to gallop at top speed and simultaneously pick up a silver coin from the ground. This game requires the participant to possess almost perfect riding skills. Kazakh folklore says that Alexander the Great, after seeing an exhibition of *kumis alu*, was so impressed that he exclaimed the game could be used in the training of a warrior on horseback. In modern games a white handkerchief is used instead of a coin.

WRESTLING

Kazakhs love wrestling. This sport has a strong Central Asian tradition, and a champion wrestler is an honored man. *Audaryspak*, or wrestling on horseback, pits both riders and their horses in close combat. The winner is the one who is able to unseat his opponent from his horse.

Two wrestlers in close combat. Wrestling, like *kokpar* and *kumis alu*, originated from the warrior tradition. In ancient times Kazakh tribes fought many battles, all on horseback. The games were a form of training for the soldiers.

BERKUTCHI

This is the sport of hunting with eagles for which Kazakhs are famous. *Berkutchi* is the name of the sport and also of the men who capture the eagles and teach them to hunt. Eagles are caught in a net trap that is baited with a small animal such as a hare. When an eagle takes the bait and flies into the net, the hunter's first job is to tie the bird's legs together to immobilize its claws. Then a small leather hood is thrown over its eyes. This usually calms the bird. Then the patient job of training the bird starts.

The hood is kept on the eagle while it becomes accustomed to the sounds, touch, and presence of people. After a week the bird is taught to take its food directly from its master's hand. As training progresses the eagle is given more freedom and is allowed to fly. The bond between bird and master grows until finally the eagle can be released and trusted to return when called. The master uses stuffed foxes to train the eagle to hunt.

Berkutchi hunt for fox with an eagle, a hound, and a horse. They ride on the steppes in search of a fox. When one is spotted, the hunter takes off the leather hood covering the bird's eyes and launches the bird into the sky. As the eagle circles in the sky and then swoops down on its prey, the hunter

A Kazakh hunter with his eagle. Hunting does not stop, even during the harsh winters.

Girls celebrating the end of a game with a song performance.

follows closely on his horse. The eagle catches the fox in its strong talons. The hunter has to be quick to call his bird back, rewarding its success with some raw meat he keeps in a little leather pouch. The hood is quickly slipped back on to calm down the bird.

Hunters can earn good money by selling fox skins. Fox hunting is a skill that is passed down from father to son, but it is a dying tradition today. Petroglyph drawings of men hunting with an eagle show that it is an ancient sport. *Berkutchi* believe that they have to keep their first kill for at least a year for good luck. One way is to have the fox fur made into a handsome hat. Eagle-hunting competitions are held during festivals.

Besides golden eagles, hunters sometimes use hawks and falcons. They also hunt other birds such as partridges, ducks, and pigeons, and animals such as hares and even wolves.

STORYTELLING

Storytelling is an important part of Kazakh tradition, going back to the days when the *akyn* or storyteller-cum-bard would journey from camp to camp to tell stories. The *akyn* would tell of the people's history or sing songs. Both adults and children looked forward to a visit from the *akyn*.

Each year is named after an animal—there is the Year of the Sheep, the Year of the Horse, the Dog, Snake, Pig, and so on. But the year that begins it all is the Year of the Mouse. This story explains how the mouse got such a prominent position.

All the animals were fighting to have their year named first. The cow said: "I give man milk, meat, and leather. I should have the first year." The horse said: "I do all that and I also give man a ride. I should have the first year." The camel said: "I am strongest and can carry any load that man gives me. The first year is mine." The sheep said: "Without my wool and felt, man would have no shelter and be cold in the winter. I want the first year." And so they quarreled until at last all the animals fell silent from tiredness. Then the little mouse, whom no one had noticed before, spoke: "I know how to solve the problem. The first animal to see the sun rise will have the first year." And they all agreed but laughed at the mouse because he was so small he surely would have no chance at all. The camel was the most confident, thinking that as he was the biggest and tallest, he would see the sun rise first. When dawn approached, all the animals faced east and waited. Suddenly they heard the mouse squeak: "I see it! I see the sun!" Without anyone realizing, the mouse had climbed up on to the camel's back so that he was highest of all. And that was how the first year in the Kazakh calendar is the Year of the Mouse.

The stories were a means of remembering the history of the Kazakhs and of teaching social values. Many stories had morals to teach, and they were often about the animals of the steppes in which these animals were endowed with human characteristics. For instance, Mouse is small but intelligent and outwits the bigger and stronger animals. Kazakh children all know about Aldar Kose, a clever and witty character who gets the better of others who are greedy or selfish by exploiting their failings. Aldar Kose is very much like Coyote, the trickster animal in Native American Indian folklore.

LEISURE TODAY

The Medeu speed-skating rink, located near Almaty, is a symbol of the modernization of Kazakhstan. The world's largest ice-skating rink, Medeu is an open-air stadium with a rink that is 1,313 feet (400 m) long. During the week it is used by ice hockey teams and world-class speed skaters, but it is open to the public on Sunday. Hundreds of skaters can then be seen swirling and tumbling across the ice. It is the site for many international competitions, and more than 100 world skating records have been broken there.

The Kazakh locals enjoy a wide variety of outdoor activities such as hiking, hunting, mountain climbing, and skiing. The town of Shymbulaq in the foothills of the Tien Shan range, near the city of Almaty, is one of Central Asia's premier ski resorts. The area is beautiful, filled with glaciers and lakes. Local residents and a growing number of tourists like to hike there.

Speed chess players at Panfilov Park in Almaty.

Hunting and fishing are also popular activities. Birds such as partridge and pheasant, fox, wolves, deer, and wild boar are all popular game. Fishing enthusiasts like to catch roach, carp, chub, and silverfish. A government license is required for fishing and hunting.

The country also offers numerous spas that are popular with both residents and tourists. These holiday resorts offer guests all sorts of medicinal treatments with curative waters.

In Almaty's Panfilov Park Kazakh men play chess in the shadow of Zenkov Cathedral. Chess is an extremely popular game among Central Asians and has been so for a very long time.

Kazakhs are becoming increasingly exposed to modern, Western culture. Movie theaters and television show American, Russian, Chinese, and Turkish movies. Rock concerts are not uncommon. Nightlife is busy especially in the capital city of Almaty.

Horse racing is another popular pastime, especially during summer weekends at the racetrack in Almaty.

FESTIVALS

A performance by the National Youth Orchestra
of Kazakhstan during a national celebration.

PUBLIC HOLIDAYS IN KAZAKHSTAN
are linked to social and political events. Because Kazakhstan is a former Soviet republic, many holidays have political significance. For instance March 8 is International Women's Day, and Victory Day, on May 9, celebrates the end of World War II for Russia.

There are no religious holidays as such, but both Christmas and the Muslim Eid al-Adha (called Kurban Ajt in Kazakh) are days when no one is expected to work, thus making them essentially holidays. Nauryz, the traditional Central Asian celebration of spring, is a recent addition to the Kazakh calendar.

Locals celebrating Christmas in church.

Although there was a suppression of Kazakh culture and tradition during Soviet times, the authorities could never really stop the feasts that accompanied the celebrations of life events in the community. Feasting and gift giving have always had great cultural significance in Kazakh society. They create ties that bind people to one another.

During the early Soviet era Nauryz was illegal. Later, the Soviet authorities decided that Nauryz could be a non-religious festival that all Soviet people in Central Asia could enjoy.

Since independence in 1991 the Kazakh government has encouraged the celebration of Nauryz as an expression of the people's national pride. The festival is the people's link to their pre-Soviet past and symbolizes a revival of tradition.

CELEBRATION OF SPRING

Nauryz is probably the most important festival of the year, celebrated by everyone in Kazakhstan, regardless of their ethnicity. It is a celebration of the coming of spring, the emergence of the first grain or sheaf of wheat, the lambing season, and the first milking. The festival is also called "the first day of the New Year" or "the great day of the people."

Rural Kazakh women decked out in their best clothes for the Nauryz celebrations in Kazakhstan.

ORIGINS OF NAURYZ

The celebration of Nauryz came to Kazakhstan through the influence of the nearby Persians many centuries ago. It is still celebrated in Iran, modern-day Persia, where it is called No Ruz *or* Norooz. *The word in the Farsi or Persian language means "new day." In Kazakhstan Nauryz is a celebration of the coming of spring and the symbolic victory of good over evil. The first No Ruz was believed to have been celebrated by the legendary Persian emperor Jamshid. Some historians think it was celebrated as long ago as in the 12th century B.C. There are many similarities in the way the Iranians and Kazakhs celebrate this festival. Since Nauryz is a time for renewal, families clean their homes to remove the previous year's dust, open their homes to everyone, buy new clothes, and visit their friends. The number seven is also important—families have a table on which they place seven objects, each beginning with the letter "S"—samanu, a sweet made of flour and sugar; sekeh, a coin; sabzee, green vegetables; sonbol, a hyacinth flower; seer, garlic; senjed, a dried fruit; and serkeh, vinegar.*

Symbols that are associated with Nauryz are the color white, which stands for goodness and riches; sweets, for abundance; and the number seven, which has a mystical significance. The traditional Nauryz dish is *kozhe*, made with seven kinds of grain, including rice, millet, and wheat. The elders of the family are ceremonially offered seven bowls of *kozhe*.

No effort is spared in this celebration, since Kazakhs believe that the more one celebrates Nauryz, the greater will be one's reward and success for the rest of the year. A lot of cooking, especially of special dishes that symbolize abundance and good tidings, is done as people visit family and friends to wish them well in the coming year. It is important that there is more than enough food and drink for all.

Although Nauryz was originally a nonreligious celebration with Persian origins, it has been given a Muslim flavor in the southern part of the country. The celebrations are blessed by the Muslim imam and presided over by the elders of the community. Celebrations begin when the New Year is greeted at noon with a prayer honoring the ancestors. This is read by the religious leader. Then the eldest in the family solemnly gives a blessing and wishes of prosperity and goodwill to everybody present.

Entertainment during Nauryz blends the modern with the traditional. In the cities Nauryz has a more secular nature. Processions, with horsemen dressing up as Kazakh heroic warriors, fill the streets, while wrestling competitions and horse races sizzle the air with excitement. Musicians perform to a lively audience, and folk singers engage in song battles.

The atmosphere during Nauryz resembles that of a carnival. In addition to the entertaining variety shows, there are stalls selling food and all kinds of merchandise.

MUSLIM CELEBRATIONS

Kazakh Muslims, like their counterparts elsewhere, observe Ramadan, the ninth month of the Islamic year, and the feast of Eid al-Fitr, also called Little Bairam or the Festival of the Breaking of the Fast, which marks the end of Ramadan. The next important Muslim celebration is Eid al-Adha, also called the Great Festival or the Festival of the Sacrifice.

Islam follows the lunar calendar, and therefore the feasts are "movable"— that is, the dates change from year to year. The first day of the month is determined by the observation of the moon by the religious authority. When the new moon of the ninth month is sighted, Ramadan begins. The holy month ends when the next new moon is seen.

Female reporters interview female Muslim pilgrims from Kazakhstan on the first day of hajj.

During Ramadan Muslims fast from sunrise to sunset, abstaining from food, drink, and tobacco, although they still carry on their normal activities. When the month is over the end of Ramadan is celebrated with the feast of Eid al-Fitr, which usually lasts for three days. During this time everyone's house is open to all friends and family. People go visiting, and there is a lot to eat and drink. Although Muslims traditionally do not drink alcohol, many Kazakh Muslims are not strict on this point, and vodka is commonly served.

Eid al-Adha is the Feast of Sacrifice and celebrates the completion of a hajj or a holy pilgrimage to Mecca, which is the holy city for all Muslims. During Eid al-Adha, all Kazakhs who can afford to will kill an animal as a sacrifice and share it in a meal with others. Families and friends visit one another on this festival.

A woman prepares a feast in her yurt for the Nauryz celebrations in Baikonur.

THE SIGNIFICANCE OF FEASTS

There are many events in a Kazakh's life that call for a feast. Births, deaths, marriages, significant birthdays—these are all celebrated with feasting, songs, and games. There are also many ceremonies for celebrating the special moments in a baby's life—when it is born, the first time it is placed on a bed, when it first stands, when it first walks, and when it is weaned.

STATE FESTIVALS IN KAZAKHSTAN

New Year, January 1

International Women's Day, March 8

Nauryz, March 21 to 23

Kazakhstan People's Unity Day, May 1

Victory Day, May 9, which commemorates the end of World War II

Capital City Day, July 6, celebrating the capital, Astana

Constitution Day, August 30, which celebrates the adoption of the new constitution in 1995

Independence Day, December 16, when Kazakhstan became independent from the Soviet Union in 1991

The *Kyrkynan shygaru* is a feast held to mark a baby's 40 days when he or she is ritually bathed and has its hair and nails cut. Before this time the young infant is confined to the bosom of the immediate family. Now it becomes a member of the larger community. *Tusau kesu* marks the time when the baby first starts to walk. The baby's feet are specially tied and a woman is chosen to cut these ties to signify this milestone in the baby's life.

Boys are often circumcised when they are between five and eight years old. It is common for a boy to be circumcised with other boys, such as his brothers or cousins. There is usually a small gathering and celebration on the day of circumcision. Guests are invited to visit with the boys in the recovery room briefly to commend them on their courage and to congratulate them for taking this important step in their life. The boys also receive gifts, often a small sum of money. Then the guests are ushered into the living room where they are offered food and drink. The big celebration is usually reserved for a later date, about a month or so later.

Preparations for a celebration begin months before the actual date. Shopping trips to the nearest city are made to buy all the items needed. Wealthy families may travel to the big cities to buy special or hard-to-get foods and gifts. Invitations are printed and sent. Gifts for the guests are picked out and set aside.

FESTIVALS TODAY

Quite apart from tradition, visitors to Kazakhstan can enjoy festivals being held all over the country. Almaty, which is alive with the arts, celebrates a Jazz Festival in the summer with performers from all over the world. The Central Asian Theater Festival brings groups from neighboring Central Asian countries such as Kyrgyzstan, Uzbekistan, and Tajikistan, which share a common tradition and culture. In Astana a Turkic Music Festival has helped revive interest in Turkic songs. Participants come from all the Central Asian Turkic-speaking nations. They perform shamanic chants, throat singing, sing epic compositions, and play songs on traditional instruments. As part of the Unity Day celebrations, Astana also hosts a Festival of Kazakhstani People meant to foster friendship among the people of Kazakhstan.

Everyone in the family is involved in the preparation. Besides the members of the immediate family, the services of friends and members of the extended family are called on. If possible, the feast is held in the yard. Tables are set up and animals slaughtered. Food is cooked over several days.

On the big day itself, guests arrive with their gifts. Gifts can range from a small piece of clothing or jewelry to a camel or a horse. As the guests are shown to their seats, a master of ceremony begins to take charge of the events of the day. The table of honor is usually the one farthest away from the entrance. This is where the person whom the feast honors sits, together with other important guests. Everyone wears his or her best clothes, whether in traditional attire or in Western dresses and suits.

If it is a wedding, the bride and groom are ushered to their seats by dancers. If it is a circumcision ceremony, then the boy is brought to the guests to be congratulated. The tables are loaded with drinks that usually include vodka, fermented mare's milk, and an endless flow of hot tea. Snacks of nuts, fruit, cookies, and candy keep everyone happy in between the main courses of soup, dumplings, pies, fried dough, and bread. Meat is present in every dish, and the richer the family, the more meat there will be. Sometimes a band is hired to provide some music. Guests listen and dance to the music and token gifts are presented to the guests who dance best or sing well. Horse races and other games are also part of the festivities, and again, the host family will have gifts to present to the winners of these games.

FOOD

People shopping for dried fruits and produce at the Zelyony Bazaar (green market).

H OSPITALITY AND GENEROSITY ARE the trademarks of the Kazakh people. A guest, whether expected or not, is always given a cordial welcome and a place of honor, and however impoverished a kitchen, the best food will be set before a guest. The respected guest is seated at the head of the table, called the *tor*.

From a young age girls are trained in the art of making a guest welcome. Be it one person or many people, the Kazakh hostess does not balk at her task.

Many different types of food are available in Kazakhstan—not only Kazakh, but also Russian, Korean, German, Chinese, Thai, and French. Kazakhs pride themselves on the cosmopolitan cuisine available in their cities.

Colorful sweets at a market stand in Almaty.

MEAT

Meat is the most important feature of any Kazakh dinner. Although Kazakhs eat a lot of mutton and beef, horse meat is prized above all and is often reserved for very special dishes. Almost all parts of the animal are eaten, including the internal organs. The heads of sheep and horses are delicacies and are offered to guests of honor.

Kazy, *zhuzhyk*, *zhaya*, *zhal*, and *karta* are all delicacies made from horse flesh. They are all either salted or smoked and boiled. *Kazy* is a sausage made of smoked meat taken from the horse's ribs. It is salted, peppered, spiced, and put into horse intestines that have been washed and cleaned in salt water. It is sometimes served sliced with hot noodles. *Zhuzhyk* is another kind of dried or smoked sausage. *Zhaya* is made from the meat of the horse's hip. *Zhal* is the fat from the underpart of the horse's neck. *Karta* is made from the horse's intestine. It is carefully washed without removing the fat and turned inside out, dried, smoked, and salted.

Shashlyk, or kebabs, are pieces of mutton and fat skewered and barbecued over a charcoal stove. They are often sold at street stalls.

The meat section of a busy indoor market in Almaty.

Fish and chicken are also part of the Kazakh diet but are not as important as beef, mutton, and horse meat. Fish comes mainly from the Caspian Sea and includes pike, perch, sprats, beluga, sturgeon, and salmon. It is usually boiled but is sometimes fried. Boiled chicken and fried fish can be served as cold appetizers before the main meat dish is presented. Caviar is a delicacy in Kazakhstan.

KAZAKH CUISINE

Kazakh cuisine is varied. Rice, vegetables and legumes, milk products, and bread are commonly eaten. Vegetables are always part of a meal, but they are seldom the main course. Radishes, carrots, potatoes, onions, peppers, and various types of green vegetables are often embellishments to meat dishes. Kazakhs like their food spiced and garnished with garlic, dill, parsley, and other herbs. *Plov* or pilaf is a rice dish and can be a simple concoction of rice, chopped mutton, and shredded vegetables fried in a large pan. A chef's version would be a fragrant combination of meat and rice, flavored with raisins and other dried fruit and the famous Kazakh apples. *Sorpa* is a soup flavored with meat or fish and served with flour dumplings or rice. *Kespe* is a soup made of meat or poultry and noodles. It is rather oily because Kazakhs love to eat the fatty parts of the meat.

Families that raise chickens also eat eggs, but they never serve them at important feasts because Kazakhs look at eggs as a poor substitute for meat.

FRIED AND FLAT BREAD

Kazakh bread is mainly in the form of flat cakes made with wheat flour, sometimes leavened with yeast. Some breads such as the *taba-nan* are baked in an oven or buried in hot charcoal. *Baursak* is a bread dough that is fried in oil. These are eaten as snacks, with sour cream and sugar, or as an accompaniment to the main meat course. *Lepeshka* is a round, unleavened bread.

Millet is another important part of the Kazakh diet. It is either pounded or used whole. Kazakhs are very inventive in their methods of cooking millet: frying it in fat, boiling it in milk, or adding it to a meat and vegetable soup to create a nourishing broth.

A Kazakh woman with the different types of breads she has baked. Bread is a staple in the Kazakh diet.

MILK FOODS

A large and important part of Kazakh cuisine consists of food made of milk and milk products. Kazakhs use the milk of all their livestock—cows, sheep, camels, horses, and goats. Those who live in the country are able to make their own butter, sour cream, yogurt, and cheese. In addition they produce many other kinds of dairy products.

The milk of an animal that has just had its young is called beestings. This milk is higher in protein and vitamins and lower in sugar and fats than milk produced later. Kazakhs differentiate three kinds of beestings. The milk immediately after calving is black beestings; the milk obtained after the calf has had its first feeding is yellow beestings; and the milk obtained 24 hours after calving is white beestings. Yellow beestings is mixed with milk, poured into a cleaned animal's stomach, and boiled with meat. White beestings is collected in a bucket, boiled, and drunk.

Irimshik is the dried curd made from the milk of a cow, sheep, or goat. Fresh milk is curdled by the addition of a rennet bag. (Rennet is the stomach of the animal that digests the curd that it chews.) The sour milk is then boiled over a low fire until the curds and whey are separated. The curd is then strained and dried in the wind and sun. It has an orange color. The whey can also be boiled slowly until a thick viscous mass is left at the bottom of the pot. This is cooled and dried in flat sheets, producing *sarysu*. *Sarysu* is sometimes called Kazakh chocolate because it supposedly tastes like chocolate.

MILK DRINKS

Kazakhs make a number of drinks from the milk of their animals. Horse and camel milk are served at wedding feasts. *Kymyz* is an alcoholic drink made from fermented mare's milk. It is a traditional drink of the nomads of Central Asia and is extremely popular. The time-honored way of making *kymyz* is to put the mare's milk into a bag made of camel or goat skin, place it in a warm spot in the yurt, and allow the natural fermentation process to take place. This usually occurs within a day. The *kymyz* is then beaten with a stick.

Shubat is fermented camel's milk. It is richer and fatter than *kymyz*. *Shubat* is made in a similar manner, and it must be stirred. *Airan* is a kind of yogurt produced from sheep's, goat's, or mare's milk.

Kazakhs believe in the medicinal and curative qualities of these milk drinks. Besides nutritional value, the drinks are believed to cure a number of digestive and intestinal problems. It is a special honor to be offered any

A woman pours *kymyz*, Kazakhstan's national drink of fermented horse milk.

A woman serving tea and food to her guests. Tea is the most popular drink in Kazakhstan. Kazakhs, whether rich or poor, are always happy to welcome guests for a feast in their homes.

of these drinks, so that it would be a social error for a guest to refuse. Guests are often asked to bless a freshly killed lamb. The spirit of the animal is asked permission to partake of its flesh, after which the meat is boiled or smoked and served with flat flour cakes and milk drinks, such as *kymyz*.

UNIVERSAL TEA

The drink that is most often found at any Kazakh meal is tea. Black tea from India and Ceylon is preferred to the cheaper loose, brick tea that comes from China. Brick tea is made from compressed tea leaves. The brick form makes it easier to transport and store. There are many qualities of brick tea; the poorest has twigs and impurities mixed with the tea leaves. The Kazakhs drink tea all the time, both as a thirst quencher and to wash down their food. Green tea is popular in the southern regions of the country where it is drunk plain without sugar or milk. Only girls and young women can pour the tea, a responsibility that seems simple but really is not. They must ensure that the tea bowls are always full and that there are no tea leaves swimming in the tea. Even if a guest protests that he has had enough to drink, it is still poor hospitality to leave his tea bowl unfilled. The hostess must offer him a *sui-ayak*, or tea bowl of honor.

Coffee, although not as popular as tea, is also a common drink. Sweet black coffee is the norm. A stronger coffee, much like Turkish coffee, is sometimes made by bringing the coffee to a boil a few times in a small coffee pot. Each time the coffee boils, it is quickly taken off the fire and a cold metal utensil like a spoon put in it to cool down the drink. This aromatic brew is served in small cups; glasses of cold water are served on the side to wash down the coffee.

ULTIMATE HOSPITALITY

The ultimate in Kazakh hospitality is the *dastarkhan*, a centuries-old tradition of receiving and serving guests. It begins with tea, often accompanied with cream, butter, jam, dried and fresh fruit, nuts, cakes, and other sweets, followed by appetizers that are usually some form of horse flesh and mutton, and vegetable tidbits.

The most honored guest is presented with the boiled head of a sheep. He is then expected to carve it and distribute the meat among the other guests present, according to their importance and station in life.

Guests are often served a rich, fragrant meaty broth, called *sorpa*, in separate bowls. Sometimes *kespe*, a noodle soup, is also served. The warm noodles are placed on a plate and a gravy of meat and vegetables is poured over them.

Finally, if they still have an appetite, guests are also free to choose from an abundant assortment of desserts. The meal is finished with more tea and the milk drink, *kymyz*.

A Kazakh family picnic in the Aksu-Zhabaghly Nature Reserve.

KAZAKH LAMB DUMPLINGS

For the filling:

1 teaspoon (5 ml) oil

¾ lb (280 g) lamb, finely minced

1 clove garlic, minced

3 tablespoons (45 ml) butter

¼ cup (60 ml) parsley, finely chopped

2 tablespoons (30 ml) cilantro, finely chopped

2 tablespoons (30 ml) salt

3 tablespoons (45 ml), boiled rice

1 egg, beaten

For the dough:

1 tablespoon (15 ml) salt

3 eggs

1 cup (250 ml) cold water

4 cups (500 ml) all-purpose flour

Dough: Combine flour and salt in a large mixing bowl. Make a deep well in the center. Add eggs and water. Mix thoroughly until the dough forms a ball. Transfer it to a lightly floured surface and flatten. Knead the dough by folding from end to end, then flattening it with the heel of your hand. Sprinkle the dough with extra flour as needed. Knead for about 15 minutes or until the dough is smooth and elastic in texture. Shape it into a ball and wrap loosely in wax paper or place in a bowl covered with a towel. Leave it to rest at room temperature for one to four hours.

Filling: Melt the butter in a large skillet. Add peanut oil and mix well over high heat. Add the lamb and garlic. Brown the meat well, making sure you break up any lumps of meat. Transfer the mixture to a bowl and add the parsley, cilantro, salt, and rice. Mix thoroughly.

Preparation: Roll the dough on a floured surface to about ⅛ inch (0.3 cm) thick. Lift and stretch it on the back of your hands until it is paper-thin. Use a glass or a cookie cutter and cut the dough into circles with a diameter of 3 inches (7.6 cm). Place a teaspoon of the filling into the center of each circle. Fold in half and press the edges of the dumpling to seal them. Lightly beat the egg. Brush the edges of the dumpling with the beaten egg. Heat the rest of the peanut oil in deep-fat fryer to 375°F (190°C). Deep fry each dumpling for two to three minutes or until they are evenly browned. Serve with rice or with soup.

GUTAP (DEEP-FRIED HERB FRITTERS)

For the filling:

1 tablespoon (15 ml) minced garlic
3 tablespoons (45 ml) chopped fresh dill
3 tablespoons (45 ml) chopped fresh parsley
9 tablespoons (135 ml) chopped scallions
1 tablespoon (15 ml) ground black pepper
8 tablespoons (120 ml) butter
1½ teaspoons (7.5 ml) salt

For the dough:

1½ cups (375 ml) all-purpose white flour
½ teaspoon (2.5 ml) salt
4 tablespoons (60 ml) softened butter
⅔ cup (167 ml) tepid water

For the sauce:

1 teaspoon (5 ml) cider vinegar
2 tablespoons (30 ml) butter
6 tablespoons (90 ml) finely minced onion
½ teaspoon (2.5 ml) salt
1 teaspoon (5 ml) ground black pepper
¼ cup (60 ml) sour cream
½ teaspoon (2.5 ml) flour
1 tablespoon (15 ml) lemon juice

Dough: Put the flour into a deep mixing bowl, making a hollow in the center of it. Slowly add the water, salt and 2 tablespoons of the butter into the hollow, stirring until the ingredients are well mixed. Beat the mixture with a wooden spoon to form a firm, stiff dough. Form the dough into a ball. Place the ball of dough onto a clean, flat surface that has been floured. Using a rolling pin, roll the dough out into a rectangular shape about 16 inches by 18 inches. Brush the dough with the remaining butter, fold it into quarters and roll it out again as evenly as possible into a large rectangle about the same size as before. Divide the dough into small 2-inch squares. You should get more than 40 little squares. With each square, place a teaspoonful of the filling in the center, and add a bit of butter. Draw up the four corners of the square, pinching them firmly together to make a little parcel enclosing the filling. Heat enough oil in a deep pot or saucepan to deep fry the parcels you have made. Drop in a few parcels at a time carefully so that you do not make a splash in the hot oil. Have an adult help you with this step if necessary. Cook each batch for about four minutes or golden brown. Remove them from the oil onto a strainer. Place on a serving dish and serve with the dipping sauce.

Filling: Combine all the ingredients except the butter, mixing well. Set aside.

Dipping sauce: Melt the butter over medium-high heat. Add the onions, salt, pepper, and vinegar. Cook for about 4 minutes. Add the sour cream and flour. Continue stirring until the sauce thickens. Remove from heat. Stir in the lemon juice and serve with the fritters.

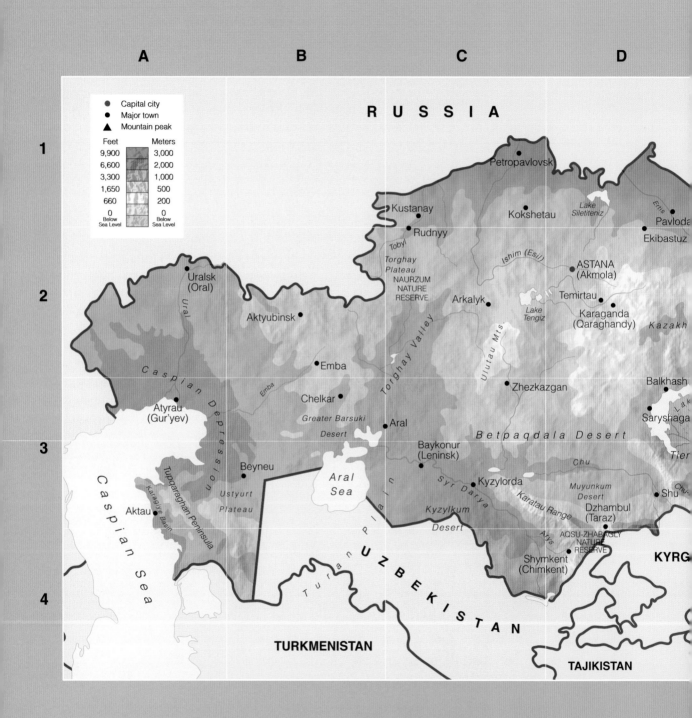

A **B** **C** **D**

1

2

3

4

RUSSIA

Capital city
Major town
Mountain peak

Feet | Meters
9,900 | 3,000
6,600 | 2,000
3,300 | 1,000
1,650 | 500
660 | 200
0 | 0
Below Sea Level | Below Sea Level

Petropavlovsk

Kustanay

Kokshetau

Lake Siletiteniz

Ertis

Pavloda

Rudnyy

Ekibastuz

Tobyl

Torghay Plateau

NAURZUM NATURE RESERVE

Ishim (Esil)

ASTANA (Akmola)

Uralsk (Oral)

Ural

Aktyubinsk

Arkalyk

Lake Tengiz

Temirtau

Karaganda (Qaraghandy)

Kazakh

Torghay Valley

Ulutau Mts.

Emba

Emba

Chelkar

Greater Barsuki Desert

Aral

Zhezkazgan

Balkhash

Saryshaga

Atyrau (Gur'yev)

Caspian Depression

Baykonur (Leninsk)

Betpaqdala Desert

Beyneu

Aral Sea

Syr Darya

Chu

Kyzylorda

Tier

Kyzylkum Desert

Karatau Range

Muyunkum Desert

Shu

Aktau

Karagiye Basin

Tupqaraghan Peninsula

Ustyurt Plateau

Turan Plain

Dzhambul (Taraz)

Caspian Sea

Shymkent (Chimkent)

Atys

AQSU-ZHABAGLY NATURE RESERVE

KYRG

UZBEKISTAN

TURKMENISTAN

TAJIKISTAN

E

Semey
Oskemen
Altai Mountains
Lake Zaysan
Chingiz-Tau Range
Upland
Ayaguz
Zaysan
Lake Alakol'
Balkhash
Lepsinsk
Dzungarian Alatau Range
aldykorgan
Shan Mountain Range
ALMATY NATURE RESERVE
Almaty
Pik Khan-Tengri
(22,958ft / 6,995m)
ZSTAN
CHINA

Aktau, A3
Almaty Nature
  Reserve, E3
Almaty, E3
Altai Mountains, F2
Aqsu-Zhabagly
  Nature Reserve,
  D4
Aral, B3, C3
Aral Sea, B3
Arkalyk, C2
Arys River, C4, D4
Astana, D2
Atyrau, A3
Ayaguz, E2

Balkhash, D3
Baykonur, C3
Betpaqdala Desert,
  C3, D3
Beyneu, B3

Caspian
  Depression,
  A2—A3, B3
Caspian Sea,
  A3—A4
Chelkar, C3
China, D4, E2—E4
Chingiz-Tau Range,
  D2, E2
Chu River, C3, D3
Chu-ily Mountains,
  D3, E3

Dzhambul, D3
Dzungarian Alatau
  Range, E3

Ekibastuz, D1—D2
Emba, B2
Emba River, B2—B3
Ertis River, D1

Greater Barsuki
  Desert, B3

Ili River, E3
Ishim River, C2, D2

Karaganda, D2
Karagiye Basin,
  A3—A4
Kazakh Upland,
  D2, E2
Kokshetau, C1
Kyrgyzstan,
  D3—D4, E3—E4
Kyzylkum Desert,
  C3—C4
Kyzylorda, C3

Lake Alakol', E2
Lake Balkhash, D3,
  E2—E3
Lake Siletitengiz, D1
Lake Tengiz, C2
Lake Zaysan, E2
Lepinsk, E3

Muyunkum Desert,
  D3

Naurzum Nature
  Reserve, C2

Oskemen, F2

Pavlodar, D1
Petropavlovsk, C1
Pik Khan-Tengri, E3

Rudnyy, C1—C2
Russia, A1—A3,
  B1—B2, C1, D1, E1

Saryshaghan, D3
Semey, E2
Shu, D3
Shymkent, D4
Syr Darya, C3

Tajikistan, D4
Taldykorgan, E3
Temirtau, D2
Tien Shan Mountain
  Range, D3, E3
Tobyl River, B2, C2
Torghay Plateau, C2
Torghay Valley, C2
Tupqaraghan
  Peninsula, A3—A4
Turan Plain, B3—B4
Turkmenistan, A4,
  B4, C4

Ulutau Mountains,
  C2—C3
Ural River, A2—A3
Uralsk, A2
Ustyurt Plateau,
  A3, B3
Uzbekistan, B3—
  B4, C3—C4, D4

Zaysan, E2
Zhezkazgan, C3

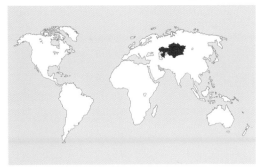

ECONOMIC KAZAKHSTAN

Services

✈ Airport

🚢 Ports

🧳 Tourism

Agriculture

🌾 Grain

🐐 Livestock

Manufacturing

🥫 Food canning

🚛 Heavy machinery

Natural Resources

C Chromium

Copper

Fishing

L Lead

Natural gas

Oil

Uranium

Z Zinc

ABOUT THE ECONOMY

OVERVIEW

After the breakup of the USSR, Kazakhstan's economy suffered a decline. The country has since been on the road to economic recovery, with its extensive fossil fuel reserves and mineral wealth being the engines taking it into the 21st century. Agriculture continues to be important, especially livestock and grain production. A unique component of Kazakhstan's economic activity is the importance of its space launch infrastructure. The Baykonur Cosmodrome, the facility built by the Soviets, continues to launch both manned and unmanned spacecraft. Due to its strong economic health and financial stability, Kazakhstan is the first Central Asian state that has been able to repay its debt to the International Monetary Fund. Several major international banks have offices in the country. Kazakhstan is a member of the Economic Cooperation Organization.

GROSS DOMESTIC PRODUCT (GDP)

$181.9 (2009 estimate)

GDP PER CAPITA

$11,800 (2009 estimate)

CURRENCY

tenge (KZT)
$1 = 147.84 KZT (2009 estimate)

INFLATION RATE

7.3 percent (2009 estimate)

LABOR FORCE

8.7 million (2009 estimate)

LABOR FORCE BY INDUSTRY

Agriculture; 31.5 percent
Industry; 18.4 percent
Services; 50 percent (2006 estimate)

UNEMPLOYMENT RATE

6.3 percent (2009 estimate)

AGRICULTURE

Grain (mostly spring wheat), cotton, livestock

NATURAL RESOURCES

Major deposits of petroleum, natural gas, coal, iron ore, manganese, chrome ore, nickel, cobalt, copper, molybdenum, lead, zinc, bauxite, gold, uranium

MAIN INDUSTRIES

Oil, coal, iron ore, manganese, choromite, lead, zinc, copper, titanium, bauxite, gold, silver, phosphates, sulfur, iron and steel, tractors and other agricultural machinery, electric motors, construction materials

MAIN IMPORTS

Machinery and equipment, metal products, foodstuffs

MAIN EXPORTS

Oil and oil products, ferrous metals, coal, chemicals, machinery, grain, wool, meat

CULTURAL KAZAKHSTAN

Steppes of Kazakhstan
The steppes stretch for more than 1,242 miles (2,000 km) from the Caspian Depression in the west to the Altai Mountains in the east. It is the largest dry steppe region in the world and can be likened to the North American prairies. This is an area of tremendous natural beauty, filled with lakes, hills, and forests. In the late 1950s much of this land was ploughed under and turned into wheat fields by hundreds of Russian and Ukrainian settlers during the Soviet Virgin Lands policy. Among the animals of the steppes are the saiga antelopes, corsac foxes, and steppe marmots.

Nauryzym nature reserve
This second-oldest reserve in Kazakhstan covers more than 214,981 acres (87,000 hectares) south of the town of Kostanai, in the Kostanai region in the north. Created to protect the unique landscape of steppes, large lake systems, and forests, the reserve is an important migration stop for the Siberian crane. Rare white herons, jack-bustards, hisser swans, and grave eagles all find sanctuary here.

Lake Balkash
One of the largest lakes in the world, the unique quality of this lake is that it contains half saltwater and half freshwater.

Semipalatinsk Test Site
West of the town of Semey, this is the site where hundreds of nuclear bomb tests were conducted in the period between 1947 and 1991.

Altyn-Emel National Park
Spreading through the Almaty oblast, the park was founded in 1961 and is especially known fo a natural phenomenon called san barkhans. These sand dunes emit singing sound when the wind blo

Baykonur Cosmodrome
A space launch facility that was built by the Soviets in the 1950s for its ambitious space program. It was from this facility that the world's first cosmonaut, Yuri Gagarin, was launched into space on April 12, 1961. The Cosmodrome is still in operation.

Tamgaly Gorge
In addition to the petroglyphs found in the Chu-Ili Mountains, this gorge also contains rock carvings, ancient settlements, and burial sites dating back to the Bronze Age.

Panfilov Park
This memorial park in Almaty was created to commemorate the 28 Kazakh soldiers who died fighting Nazi tanks in a village outside Moscow in 1941. Also in the par is Zenkov Cathedral, built in 1907, a larg wooden church built without using a singl nail. During Soviet times it was turned int a concert hall and museum. Today it has regained use as a house of worship.

Karagie Depression
At 433 feet (132 m) below sea level, this is the second-lowest point in the world after the Dead Sea. The landscape is rocky desert land and drifting sands. The 12th to 14th century Shakpak-Ata Mosque, hewn out of rock, is an attraction of this area.

Kodja Ahmed Yasavi Mausoleum
One of Islam's most important pilgrimage sites in Central Asia, the site is located in Turkistan, 102 miles (165 km) northwest of Shymkent in the Syr-Darya valley. Kodja Ahmed Yasavi was the first great Turkic Muslim holy man, Sufi teacher, and mystical poet. He had tremendous influence in the Turkic-speaking world. The mausoleum was built by Timur, the 14th-century conqueror.

Aksu-Zhabagly Nature Reserve
Located in South Kazakhstan, at the western extremity of the Western Tien Shan Mountains, this UNESCO World Heritage area is home to hundreds of species of birds, animals, and plants. It covers a variety of landscapes, from the dry semi-desert, to steppes, forests, and alpine meadows. It is honored as the home of the tulip.

Tien Shan ('Heavenly Mountains')
This mountain range stretches on more than 932 miles (1,500 km). It has the two highest peaks in the land—Pobeda Peak (24,406 feet/7,439 m) and Khan-Tengri Peak (23,000 feet/7,010 m). Although it is the second-highest point, the Khan-Tengri Peak is better known for the beautiful white, marble-like countenance that it presents. It truly anchors the southeast corner of the country.

ABOUT THE CULTURE

OFFICIAL NAME
Republic of Kazakhstan

DESCRIPTION OF FLAG
Sky-blue background with a gold sun with 32 rays above a golden eagle in the center. The hoist side of the flag has a yellow design called a "national ornamentation."

TOTAL AREA
1,048,878 square miles (2,717,300 square km)

CLIMATE
continental, cold winters and hot summers, arid and semiarid

CAPITAL
Astana

POPULATION
15,460,484 (2010 estimate)

GOVERNMENT
Republic; authoritarian presidential rule, with little power outside the executive branch

LIFE EXPECTANCY
Total population: 68.19 years
Male: 62.91 years
Female: 73.78 years (2010 estimate)

BIRTHRATE
16.66 births/1,000 population (2010 estimate)

DEATH RATE
9.39 deaths/1,000 population (2010 estimate)

LITERACY RATE
99.5 percent (2010 estimate)

MAJOR RELIGIONS
Islam 47 percent, Russian Orthodox 44 percent, Protestant 2 percent, other 7 percent.

ETHNIC GROUPS
Kazakh (Qazaq) 63.6 percent, Russian 23.3 percent, Ukrainian 2.0 percent, Uzbek 2.9 percent, German 1.1 percent, Tatar 1.2 percent, Uyghur 1.4 percent, other 4.5 percent (2009 estimate)

MAIN LANGUAGES
Kazakh (or Qazaq, the state language) 64.4 percent, Russian (official language used in everyday business, designated the "language of interethnic communication") 95 percent (2001 estimate).

COMMUNICATIONS
Mobiles: 14.9 million (2008 estimate)
Internet: 2.3 million (2008 estimate)

TIME LINE

IN KAZAKHSTAN	IN THE WORLD
1st century A.D. Central Asia is settled by Turkic-speaking and Mongol tribes.	**A.D. 116–17** Roman Empire reaches its greatest extent under Emperor Trajan.
8th–9th centuries Parts of southern Kazakhstan are conquered by Arabs. Arabs introduce Islam into the area.	
11th–12th centuries Tribal powers fight among themselves for control of the area.	**1206–1368** Genghis Khan unifies the Mongols and starts conquest of the world. At its height, the Mongol Empire under Kublai Khan stretches from China to Persia and parts of Europe and Russia.
1219–24 Genghis Khan and his Mongol tribes invade Kazakhstan and Central Asia.	
15th century Kazakhs emerge as a recognizable group.	**1530** Beginning of the transatlantic slave trade organized by the Portuguese in Africa
17th century Kazakhstan comes under the control of three tribal federations: the Great Horde, Middle Horde, and Lesser Horde.	**1620** Pilgrims sail the *Mayflower* to America.
1645 Russians set up an outpost on the north coast of the Caspian Sea.	
18th–19th century Russians are in firm control of the Kazakh tribes.	**1789–99** The French Revolution
19th century The three hordes are abolished; Russian military rule is established.	
1837 Beginning of the revolts against Russian rule, first led by Khan Kene	
1847 Khan Kene is killed.	
1906–12 Thousands of Russian and Ukrainian farmers settle the land.	**1914** World War I begins.
1916 Kazakhs resist Russian attempt to recruit them in the fight against Germany.	**1917** Civil war breaks out in Russia following the Bolshevik Revolution.
1920 Kazakhstan becomes an autonomous republic of the USSR.	
Late 1920s–1930s Agriculture is collectivized. Kazakh nomadic lifestyle is discouraged and more than a million Kazakhs and most of the country's livestock die.	

IN KAZAKHSTAN	IN THE WORLD
1936 Kazakhstan becomes a Soviet republic.	
1940s Forced resettlements to Kazakhstan of Koreans, Crimean Tatars, Germans, and others	**1945** The United States drops atomic bombs on Hiroshima and Nagasaki. World War II ends.
1949 First nuclear test explosion conducted at Semipalatinsk.	
1954–65 Virgin Lands policy of Nikita Khrushchev saw the planting of steppe lands with wheat.	**1957** The Russians launch Sputnik, the world's first artificial satellite.
1985 Dinmukhamed Kunayev is forced to resign as leader of the Communist Party of Kazakhstan (CPK) in favour of Gennadiy Kolbin.	**1986** Nuclear power disaster at Chernobyl in Ukraine
1989 Nursultan Nazarbayev is made head of the CPK.	
1991 Kazakhstan declares independence and joins the Commonwealth of Independent States.	**1991** Breakup of the Soviet Union
1993 A new constitution is adopted replacing the Soviet constitution. Kazakh is made the state language; Russian is the language of communication.	
1997 The capital of Kazakhstan is moved from Almaty to Akmola. Later Akmola is renamed Astana.	**1997** Hong Kong is returned to China.
2001 A major pipeline from the Tengiz oil field transports oil to the Russian Black Sea port of Novorossiysk. In December President Nazarbayev and U.S. president George Bush declare their commitment to a long-term, strategic partner	**2001** World population surpasses 6 billion; Terrorists crash planes into New York, Washington D.C., and Pennsylvania on September 11
2005 The newly formed Democratic Choice reform movement comes into increasing conflict with President Nazarbayev's government. The court orders the dissolution of Democratic Choice. Later in the year President Nazarbayev is returned as president for another term in office in elections criticized as flawed.	**2003** War in Iraq begins. Space shuttle *Columbia* explodes, killing all seven astronauts aboard.
2009 The Kazakh section of a natural gas pipeline linking the country to China is unveiled.	**2009** Barack Obama becomes the first African-American president of the United States.

GLOSSARY

akyn (ar-KERN)
Kazakh folk singer or storyteller.

circumcision
Cutting off the foreskin of the male penis.

Commonwealth of Independent States (CIS)
An organization composed of former Soviet republics: Armenia, Azerbaijan, Belarus, Georgia, Kirgyzstan, Moldovia, the Russian Federation, Tajikistan, Turkmenistan, the Ukraine, and Uzbekistan.

horde
A clan or group of nomadic Central Asian people who claim hunting and grazing rights over an area.

intelligentsia
A group of educated people forming a distinct social class in society.

jyrau (JAI-rau)
Kazakh lyric poet.

Khan
The ruler of a Central Asian tribe.

nomads
A group of people who travel from place to place in a seasonal pattern to give their animals grazing grounds.

Politburo
The main political and executive committee of the Communist Party.

shaman
A person who is believed to have the power to cure the sick, divine the future, and act as an intermediary between the people and the spirits.

Slav
A member of an ethnic and linguistic group of people in Eastern Europe—for example, Russians, Ukrainians, and Belorussians.

steppes
Vast and grassy plains found in parts of Europe, Asia, and the United States.

Turkic
A linguistic subgroup of the Altaic family of languages, and a term to describe the people who speak these languages.

Union of Soviet Socialist Republics (USSR)
Also called the Soviet Union, the USSR was established as a result of the 1917 Russian Revolution. From 1940 to 1990 it consisted of 15 European and Asian republics. It broke up in 1991.

yurts
Dome-shaped felt tents used by nomads.

FOR FURTHER INFORMATION

BOOKS

Aitken, Jonathan. *Nazarbayev and the Making of Kazakhstan: From Communism to Capitalism.* London: Continuum Pub Group, 2010.

Olcott, Martha Brill. *Kazakhstan: Unfulfilled Promise.* Washington, D.C.: Carnegie Endowment for International Peace, 2010.

Robbins, Christopher. *Apples are from Kazakhstan: The Land that Disappeared.* New York: Atlas & Co, 2010.

Schreiber, Dagmar. *Kazakhstan: Nomadic Routes from Caspian to Altai* (Odyssey Illustrated Guides). Hong Kong: Odyssey Publications, 2010.

FILMS

Sergei Dvortsevoy. *Tulpan.* Zeitgeist Films, 2009.

Gulshat Omarova. *Schizo.* Picture This! Home Entertainment, 2005.

MUSIC

Various. *Kazakhstan : Music From Almati,* Gallo, 1996.

Various. *Dombra From Kazakhstan 2,* Buda Records, 2010.

BIBLIOGRAPHY

BOOKS

Brummell, Paul. *Kazakhstan* (Bradt Travel Guide). Bucks, U.K.: Bradt Travel Guides, 2008.

Dave, Bhavna. *Kazakhstan: Ethnicity, Language and Power.* Oxford, U.K.: Routledge, 2008.

Edwards-Jones, Imogen. *The Taming of Eagles, Exploring the New Russia.* London: Weidenfeld & Nicolson, 1993.

Glenn, E. Curtis, ed. *Kazakhstan: A Country Guide.* Washington, D.C.: Library of Congress, Federal Research Division, 1996.

WEBSITES

CIA World Factbook—Kazakhstan. www.cia.gov/library/publications/the-world-factbook/geos/kz.html

For statistics on Kazakhstan. www.eng.stat.kz/Pages/default.aspx

Good overall information on the country, meant for travelers. http://aboutkazakhstan.com/Taraz_city.shtml

Internet portal of the Government of Kazakhstan. http://e.gov.kz/wps/portal/home?lang=en

Kazakhstan's Echo, a publication of the embassy of Kazakhstan. www.kazakhembus.com

KazakhstanLive.com, international information center of Kazakhstan. www.kazakhstanlive.com/5en.aspx?sr=4

News on Kazakhstan. www.inform.kz/eng/content/123

Parliament website for number of deputies in Senate and Mazhilis. www.parlam.kz/Information.aspx?lan=en-US

U.S. energy information administration website with information on oil production in Kazakhstan. www.eia.doe.gov/cabs/Kazakhstan/Oil.html

U.S. Department of State website on Kazakhstan. www.state.gov/r/pa/ei/bgn/5487.htm

Website of families with children adopted from Kazakhstan. www.kazakhadoptivefamilies.com/index.html

Website of the embassy of the Republic of Kazakhstan in the United States. www.kazakhembus.com/index.php?page=alias

INDEX

INDEX